MY STORY, YOUR HOPE

WHEN FEAR, PAIN, LOSS, AND GRIEF ARE TOO MUCH TO IGNORE

AN ANTHOLOGY

Dr. Michelle Kindred

Foreword By Dr. Cheryl Polote-Wiliamson

Cocoon to Wings
PUBLISHING

MY STORY, YOUR HOPE

Copyright © 2024 Donna Michelle Kindred

Printed in the United States of America
ISBN: 978-1-963964-01-1 (Paperback)
ISBN: 978-1-963964-02-8 (Digital)
Library of Congress Control Number: 2024906416
Published by Cocoon to Wings Publishing
7810 Gall Blvd, #311
Zephyrhills, FL 33541
www.CocoontoWingsBooks.com
(813) 906-WING (9464)

Book design by ETP Creative

Dr. Michelle Kindren's photos used with permission from **Reflections HD Photography**. (ReflectionsHD.com)

Dr. Michelle Kindred

Foreword by Dr. Cheryl Polote-Williamson

MY STORY, YOUR HOPE

WHEN FEAR, PAIN, LOSS, AND GRIEF ARE TOO MUCH TO IGNORE

AN ANTHOLOGY

Dedication

Giving all honor and glory to my Lord and Savior, Jesus Christ, for his faithfulness, for pushing me into purpose, and for keeping me.

To every woman who, like me, has felt the sting of not feeling good enough. To every woman who, like me, has a wealth of potential inside but struggles to bring it to the surface. To every woman who, like me, may not have fully realized that they are seen, heard, and significant. To every woman who, like me, battles with self-doubt, perfectionism, toxic relationships, or unwise plans and circumstances.

To every woman, remember that you are never alone. Your journey has a purpose. By focusing on God and trusting his plan for our lives, we stand together, supporting each other through the mountains and valleys in the darkest times, lowest points, and most challenging situations. "Many are the plans in a person's heart, but it is the Lord's purpose that prevails," Proverbs 19:21 (NIV).

To everyone with a story. Whether blissful and true or painfully traumatic, our past shapes who we are today. The art of storytelling is a process that can heal the brokenhearted, revive the oppressed, and rebirth purpose from fire. **You** have a story;

write it down and make it plain. *(paraphrased, Habakkuk 2:2 NKJV)*

To my co-authors, you are seen, heard, and significant! You are the epitome of a phoenix.

With love and respect,

Just write,

Dr. Michelle

Foreword

Dr. Michelle Kindred is much more than a survivor. With her faith in God, perseverance, selflessness, and unwavering love for others, she has turned her trials into undeniable triumphs that have proven to be inspirational for countless women. In doing so, she felt God calling her to compile the stories of other inspirational women. In this soul-stirring, power-packed anthology, you will discover that you can survive hardships and you can thrive after overcoming them! In this book, you will read the testimonies of 12 amazing women who have weathered various storms of life, including the death of a child, the death of a spouse, and domestic violence. You will also read stories about self-discovery, healing, and recovering from the mental and emotional trauma of Superwoman Syndrome and living an authentic and purpose-centered life. Regardless of where you are on your journey, there is something here for you.

One of the most common feelings that we experience when we are in a challenging chapter of our lives is the feeling of isolation. The life-changing stories that you are about to read are proof that you are not alone and that you never were alone. God has an uncanny way of aligning our paths with others who have experienced similar situations. In doing so, He confirms that we are not alone and that there is an important lesson in every struggle. The fact that you are currently holding this book is a perfect example of divine alignment in action. God wants us to know that there is a lesson in every loss, disappointment, heartbreak, and setback. The challenge is for us to learn the lessons and use them as fuel to make us better, stronger, and more compassionate and to become beacons of light and hope for others whom we meet along the way.

As you read each testimony, I hope you gain hope and confidence knowing that you can and will thrive. You can use the lessons of your experiences and the experiences of others to become the best version of yourself. My prayer for you is that you remember that God's love for you is unending. I hope you remember that validation is for parking, not people, for when God made you, He said you were good! I hope each testimony inspires you to turn your pain into passion and purpose. I hope these stories minister to you and remind you that you already have the tools you need to overcome. These stories were written and compiled with you in mind. Be blessed, and remember that you are loved and supported, always.

DR. CHERYL POLOTE-WILLIAMSON
BESTSELLING AUTHOR
FILMMAKER
MOTIVATIONAL SPEAKER
LIFE COACH
PHILANTHROPIST

Prologue

GODSpired

I woke up every day for about a year with a nagging feeling telling me to share my story and thoughts. I didn't understand why. I remember thinking, "What story? Why should I share it?" I believed that I was okay and that it wasn't a big deal to share. But the thought kept coming back to me. It was a burning desire to be heard and seen. After praying and meditating on it, I realized it was not my conscience tugging at me; it was the Holy Spirit.

I knew I needed to be obedient, even though I wanted to dismiss the thought. Being human, I questioned God, saying, "Why would my story mean anything to anyone? I'm probably the only one who thinks what I've been through is significant." But God revealed to me that I was not alone in my feelings and that many strong, educated, beautiful, and successful women have stories to tell, and it's important for others to see that even if the journey may seem desolate, the results can be strengthening. Like me, many of us wear masks and keep up appearances so that no one knows what we've gone through. Pushing past the hesitation, I said yes to God and yes to the project.

My Story, Your Hope, Is not just an anthology but a project of cleansing, acknowledgment, and healing. Sometimes, we smooth over the pain of our stories and avoid reliving the details, or we block the connecting pieces that define our current state of being. We focus on the happy ending and eliminate the risk of opening old wounds or filling the gaps that connect the past and the present.

As the authors of each story were tasked with putting their stories to paper, they faced head-on challenges, demons, and fears as they not only relived each component of their story but also found themselves submerged in a myriad of emotions, readdressing issues and combating hidden truths. Some authors made pivoting connections and helped heal others within their stories. At the same time, others removed the blinders and found further healing for themselves.

The authors were committed to giving you a bold, intense experience, allowing you to feel each step in the journey with strategies, tips, prayer, and Godly references.

My Story, Your Hope, will take you on the journey of thirteen women, just like you, with their individual and unique stories, filled with components of love, loss, grief, and pain, vividly written to give you a candid peek into the trials, turmoil, release, and healing of a journey that is widely similar but often suppressed by many.

My Story, Your Hope. The story must be shared when fear, pain, loss, and grief are too much to ignore. Take a moment and write your story down, validate your feelings, and make the connections between past and present. Healing is in sharing.

DR. MICHELLE KINDRED

Table of Contents

Dr. Tiffany M. Crayton, Ph.D., LPC, NCC, DARTT

 Dr. Tiffany Marie Crayton is, first and foremost, a child of God who believes that she is not where she is because of what she has done; however, because of the hand of God. Dr. Tiffany is a clinical psychotherapist who owns a thriving private practice, Inspired Purpose Counseling & Consulting, in Virginia. It is in this practice that she does the heart work with marginalized populations who are overcoming traumatic events and discovering their inherent worth. She helps others find the beauty in their brokenness to help propel them boldly into their purpose.

She utilizes over 20 years of mental health experience with a specialty in trauma to train companies on imposture syndrome, racial trauma, generational trauma, and other phenomenon that impact women of color and marginalized populations. She serves as a college professor who is committed to training and challenging emerging clinicians to do their own work so they can show up as their true, authentic, healed selves in their counseling spaces to assist those they serve in their healing journey.

Dr. Tiffany is a survivor of intimate partner violence and is committed to helping other women and men overcome the pain and loss experienced through surviving abuse. She is the host of an upcoming podcast called "Empowered by Fire," which is a platform dedicated to giving voice to others who have overcome insurmountable challenges. She is the author of a soon-to-be-published book by the same name. She is the wife of her knight in shining armor, Kevin, and mother of two AMAZING black men, Caleb and Cameron, and "Nani" to Canaan and Joshua.

Empowered by Fire

Tiffany M. Crayton

*"You cannot see my scars or the scorch of the flames,
for God protected and preserved me.
I don't look like what I have been through."*

My regular Sunday morning routine was abruptly distorted. I would typically prepare for church and my all-time joy of singing on the praise and worship team. Instead, my joy was damaged as I looked in the mirror to see a plum-sized and colored bruise around my left eye. "You are ugly, no one will ever want you, you're pathetic," are the words from him that replayed in my head like a broken record. With all my strength, I was determined to get ready for church. Maybe this was my way of hoping someone would see through the scars and inquire about my well-being. I covered my left eye with what seemed like an entire bottle of concealer. Taking a final look in the mirror to double check if the bruise was still visible. What looked back at me was what I always swore I would never become... my mother.

He was the total package: tall, with creamy caramel skin, athletic, always well-dressed, and charismatic. Every girl wanted

3

him. Two months into the relationship, those suave characteristics soon faded into what appeared to be the textbook signs of a narcissist.

He would often accuse me of cheating on him with family members or the guy at the mall who may have given me an innocent stare. I was always "F*****g" someone, let him tell it, but it was him that was cheating. It was the moment when we came home from a family party and he accused me of sleeping with his cousin, that I knew things were getting out of control.

Despite the signs and my uneasiness, I listened to others tell me, "Girl, this is the man," or "He's a Godsend." We were married by the end of the year.

I thought surely things would get better. We were now married, and if I did the things he wanted me to and acted the way he suggested, I could make it work. All I had to do was make sure he wasn't upset about anything. Perhaps if I prayed more, if I increased my faith, if I worked harder, if I did more of the things he wanted me to do, things would get better. Perhaps me loving him harder would change him. You may be thinking, *"Really, things get better?"* You're right! It only got worse. By that point, I was pregnant with our first son. I assumed that my being pregnant would change things. It didn't. And five years later, not planned, but by force, I was pregnant with baby number two.

I became unsure of who I was because I had been in this relationship long enough for him to distort how I once saw myself. I trusted more of what they [the women of the church] said God was saying to them than what the Holy Spirit was saying to me. I questioned my faith and believed everyone deserved a second chance.

His behavior persisted; he became more controlling. There were countless encounters where he would grab me and shake me. That progressed into pushing me down a flight of stairs, punching me in the face, and fighting me like a man. I had breaks and bruises in places I hate to mention.

I have buried this story so deep in my soul because of shame and the inability to realize how I could have ended up in a volatile marriage that lasted close to 12 years and almost cost me my life. He held a Glock 9mm handgun to my head while yelling derogatory names. "You cheating ass bitch! I don't even know why I am with your ass! What are you going to do, leave me? Nobody will want you!"

While he continued to berate me, I wept while fear consumed every part of my being. However, as he began to cock the gun to ensure the bullets were in the chamber, I began to feel calm in my thoughts - *this could be my way out*. All the beatings would stop. No more black eyes to cover up. No more broken bones from being pushed down the stairs, no more bruises hidden where no one could see. No more marital rape. The repeated words of not being good enough, being a sorry-ass wife would be silenced. There were parts of me that wanted him to pull the trigger. As he pressed the gun into my right temple, with my eyes tightly shut, I began to think about my son. I began to think how his life would be if he did not have me to raise him. I called on the name of Jesus. I held my breath, braced myself for my anticipated demise with tears and sweat streaming down my face, my husband pulled the trigger.

When the bullet did not discharge, I fell to the ground and exhaled with great relief. My ex-husband was enraged. He yanked me up from the floor and put the gun back to my head. During this time of terror, I made a promise to God that if He let me live, I would share my story with other women and snuff out death, discouragement, and despair. For a second time, the bullet did not discharge. Since he could not kill me, he decided he would rape me instead. As I lay on my back, forced to feel him inside of me, I prayed to God and wept until he finished violating me. Not long after this incident, another attempt to leave him, and another beating, his mother told me, "If you do not leave him, he will kill you." As a young mother, I wondered how hard it was for her to secretly say those words about her own child.

It wasn't until my youngest son, who was three years old at the time, became more aware of the things that were happening between me and his father that I knew I had to do something. He witnessed personal attacks like his father berating me, spitting on me, breaking sentimental things, and kicking me at will. I didn't want him to think this was how a man should treat a woman. After seeing the look in my son's eyes, I knew I had to leave. During this last outrage, I ran out of the house, grabbing both boys and fled to a neighbor's house. We stayed there until I filed a VPO – victim protective order, and the police removed him from the home. Once we got back into the house, I began the process of filing for divorce.

Due to fear, embarrassment, and shame, I have not upheld my promise to God until now. Ironically, all throughout my marriage, I worked in the behavioral sciences field. I finished my master's degree and began working as a high school counselor. About ten years after the divorce, I went back to graduate school to pursue a Ph.D. in Counseling Education and Supervision with a concentration in Trauma. One would think I would be well-versed and healed through all this schooling.

Having been a living example of my studies, I questioned how I could help anyone out of a depressed state, low self-esteem, or anxiety when I had experienced all these things myself. God did not see me that way at all. My past and all that I endured would not forfeit my purpose.

The truth is I was so bound to him through the abuse I did not know how to get out of the entangled mess. I did not trust myself, nor did I trust God's love for me. I had developed sympathy for the one who was abusing me while forsaking compassion for myself. Disturbingly, when I would share my story, I would hear comments such as "You must like getting hit, because there is no way I would let someone treat me the way you were being treated." "What did you do? You must have done something to upset him." "Why didn't you just leave?" "Strong Black women don't allow men to beat them. You must be weak."

I often felt there was something I did to deserve the pain being inflicted upon me through emotional, psychological, and physical abuse. At times, I felt the abuse was God's way of punishing me for not listening to His voice. Who walks into a marriage believing they will become divorced? We were a good-looking couple. We presented well. Most admired us because we fit the part of the ideal church couple. What a failure I would be if I exposed the truth of what was happening. But if I were dead, what would it matter? I would be another woman who died at the hands of her intimate partner. I would leave two sons who would be emotionally scarred for the rest of their lives. Or I could figure out a way with God's help.

I did try to leave several times after the gun incident. I found it difficult to find resources that would not disrupt the normalcy of my sons' lives. Yes, normalcy. But what was normal about living in a home where violence was so prevalent it was like talking about the weather? I chose to stay because, as crazy as it sounds, it was better to stay in a hell that I knew than to expose my sons to a hell I didn't know.

I prayed to God to help me make a way of escape for me and my boys. Part of this plan was to finish my master's degree and licensure to provide a good quality of life for my sons. This is not what I would recommend for women in volatile relationships; however, it is what was best for me. I knew that finishing my education would give us access to a life that we would not have if I did not complete it. During this time in my life, the trauma bonding was in full force. I had no idea how to leave someone who was so consumed with themself. I found myself in a marriage I never dreamed of being in. It was not marital bliss at all. It was nothing like I saw in the movies. I wish I had loved myself more and trusted the God that ruled and reigned in my life. Anyone and everyone that meant anything to me, he found something wrong with. He would say negative things about them so much that I began to believe the false narratives I would witness about someone's behavior. He was the king of gaslighting. Before I realized it, I was alone. He was my only friend. He would choose who was okay for me to interact with. Be sure to pay attention to the subtle signs of isolation, control, and manipulative behavior. They do not want you around anyone who can see through them and their tactics. These are typically the signs of a narcissist. Although I never knew from one day to the next if it was going to be a spit, hit, or kick day, I asked God to preserve me. To keep me and my boys safe. To make a way of escape for me. I did not want myself or my sons to look like what we had been through. More importantly, I did not want them to believe that treating women the way they saw their father treat me was appropriate. I prayed this prayer long before I heard these words in a song. Although I have many regrets about the humiliation I endured, I genuinely believe if it had not been for my two sons, I would be dead. They gave me the strength to fight my way out of that marriage so I could save them; however, in the process, they saved me.

God gave me a way of escape. One may ask: how did you heal from such a tumultuous marriage? I am still healing. Anytime you have experienced a form of trauma, you keep moving, and you stay busy because, in your busyness, you do not allow yourself to feel. This is a trauma response. I did not begin my healing journey until the world shut down from COVID-19. Not only were we fighting against a viral infection that could potentially kill us, but I was also sitting in the pain of years of abuse. As a clinician, I attended trauma training, and part of the training was facing your own trauma. Through the 18-month training, I began to take steps toward my healing. In addition to surrounding myself with positive, God-fearing human beings that poured into me, and I into them, I prayed for God to preserve me. I did not want to look like the pain I had endured. I did not want my body to be representative of the punches I absorbed throughout my life but to be a visible testament of God's power.

I am like the three Hebrew boys in the fiery furnace. What was meant to destroy me and leave me for dead could not match the power of God's favor on my life. What I have learned is that when I began to see God the way He sees me, my walk was different. How I talk is different. I am more intentional in how I treat others, how I speak about myself, and how I enter certain spaces. I realize that I do not have to make myself small because others cannot hold space for the light that rules and reigns in my life. When you operate in this manner, there is no room for shame. What I know now is that God chose me - a battered, broken vessel - and since He chose me, I have nothing to be ashamed of. My courage in Him is always going to produce the best.

Reflection:

How do you find the courage to walk towards your purpose even when it doesn't make sense?

What is it within you that will not allow you to fully surrender and trust God?

Affirmative Prayer:

"Trust in the Lord with all your heart and lean not on your own understanding; in all your ways submit to him, and he will direct your path." Proverbs 3:5-8 (NLT)

Just Write

Dr. Rita Hunt-Anderson

Dr. Rita Hunt-Anderson is a community activist, bereavement educator, and loss and grief coach. She is a professor of Death and Dying courses and advanced education studies. Her groundbreaking work supports those who experience the various stages of grief, such as denial, isolation, depression, bargaining, anger, and acceptance. Dr. Anderson speaks internationally on death and dying, tailoring recovery methods to each individual and situation. Her motto is, "There is no one size fits all when it comes to grieving."

Dr. Anderson continues to support those recovering from the pain associated with grief by providing weekly group guidance and activities for families, individual coaching sessions, and community service. In honor of her son, she founded the nonprofit *When Is Now Foundation (WIN)*, where she assists, educates and leads groups for those coping with loss and grief. *WIN* underscores her commitment to helping others deal with the desolation of death.

She continues to be a part of bereavement circles, working for Keiser Permanente and volunteering at various community centers. She believes that grief and its related journey, while it can be overwhelming, you need not feel alone.

Tears in Heaven

Rita Hunt-Anderson

"Weeping may endure for a night, but joy cometh in the morning."

PSALM 30:5 (KJV)

"Stop, look, and listen,
Before you cross the street!
Use your eyes, use your ears, And then use your feet!"

This refrain from a children's song haunted me for months after my son William's death. I wondered if it had been the one song I should've remembered to include in our nightly ritual of lullabies and bedtime stories. I wondered whether he might still be alive if I had taught him this safety chant. Would he have said to himself, as the other children were playing in the street, "Stop! Don't go out there!"

William, or Will as I sometimes called him, was an active nine-year-old who was tall for his age. He loved measuring his height against mine. Each time, he'd say, "Mom, I think I grew a little. I'm almost bigger than you."

15

He'd grab my hand and lead me to his room and open the closet door where we kept track of how much he'd grown. There were hash marks and dates from the time he was able to walk. Behold, he was right; he had grown nearly half an inch within the last six months.

Sometimes I'd ask him, "Who are you?"

Will would answer, "Mama, I am your sunshine. Don't you know that?"

It was our call and answer to affirm our love for each other. William knew I loved the sunshine; the rays made me feel alive, and he associated it with happiness.

He was talented, an excellent swimmer, and somewhat popular in school, especially with the girls; they loved his long eyelashes. Will was smart; he'd be the first to turn in his assignments and would rarely have homework. However, he wasn't always intent on following his teacher's instructions. Since the divorce, I noticed a more distracted William. His teacher would stop me at the parent-pickup line and say, "He doesn't listen," "He seems restless," or "He's really having a hard time focusing." I knew this restlessness was typical behavior for a kid whose parents were splitting up.

Divorce was never part of my grand plan. I'm the oldest of four girls and the product of a broken home. For as long as I can remember, I've always felt like the second mother to my younger sisters. Parenting early, having responsibilities, and taking charge came easily to me. When my parents divorced, my mother worked two jobs to support our family. We lived in a great neighborhood and were a financial step above what one might expect from a single-parent home. But Mom was a warrior, and I learned how to *do* it by watching her. I also learned that divorce is hard on everyone. I remember thinking that I would never put my own family through anything so traumatic.

By the time I entered high school, I was tired of being responsible, and I carefully planned my escape. My plan:

- Graduate early from high school.
- Push through college.
- Find a husband.

I was married at twenty-one and couldn't wait to start a family. I wanted to be a mother to my **own** children and have a happy little family. In hindsight, in my opinion, my husband was not in the same place in life as me. I think he was ignoring his inner voice, probably whispering, "You're not ready to be a father." But his actions spoke much louder.

Not long after we were married, my husband started to act very immature. He'd hang out with his friends and come home late or not at all. In retrospect, his behavior wasn't so different from how he'd acted before we were married; the problem was that I thought he'd grow up and become more of a husband and, eventually, a father. I should have paid attention to the signs all around me that reinforced the adage, "*People don't change.*" For the next two years, there was more of the same irresponsible behavior. I became pregnant but thought things would be okay. Surely, he would come to his senses since I was pregnant. The disagreements, fighting, and his disappearing for days escalated.

I always expected that my husband would be there for our family, especially for our child. I wasn't aiming for perfection, but I did want him to be a participating partner. As we neared our son's birth, still trying to force this unity, I would say things like,

"We need to get the baby's room ready. What colors should we paint? Do you want to video the birth?" Crickets.

I could have prepared it myself, but I wanted to share the experience of getting ready for a baby together. It wasn't until our son was born that my husband said, "We'd better get a crib."

"Ya think?" I mumbled under my breath. This was definitely not the partner I'd so desperately wanted.

After ten years of trying, my husband and I went our separate ways. I went back home to my mother, and he moved to the East Coast to be close to his sister and nephews; I guess he thought he would be a male role model for them. I remember shaking my head in disbelief at that notion. We did manage to work out visitation rights for our son. William loved his father and watching us fall apart was especially hard on him. It was hard on everyone.

The first summer William visited his father, he was nine years old. I had put it off as long as I could. The day he boarded the plane, my maternal instinct told me to keep him safe with me. But my ex had legal rights to time with Will, and Will wanted to see his father, so I had no choice in the matter.

My husband had his friends over for an afternoon barbecue during the last week before William was to return home. From what his sister told me, a group of kids was playing in front of the house while the adults were out back. Where I'm from, one adult always stays fully alert during such events and checks on the kids. I don't think anybody checked that day.

Meanwhile, I was at home, enjoying a leisurely day of shopping with my best friend. For some reason, I had left my phone at home. Probably when I changed purses, I'd left it on the dresser. I wasn't worried; I figured I'd run by to get it after lunch. Oddly, I bought all-black clothes that day: a black dress, a handbag, and matching shoes. This was bizarre since I usually bought bright colors. We returned home at about 2:00 p.m. Checking my phone, there were several missed calls from my ex-husband, my mom, and my cousin. They'd called earlier that morning. I started listening to the voicemails, "Call as soon as possible," "Something has happened to Will," the messages said.

When I called my mom first, "Something has happened to Will. Have you talked to Jamie [my ex]?"

I replied, "No, why?"

She repeated, "We lost him. We lost him ..."

As I attempted to call my ex-husband, another call was coming through; It was my cousin BeBee. I answered, and she was frantic, shouting, "Will is gone, Will is gone."

Nobody mentioned the word dead, so I assumed he'd gone missing. I said, "Okay, okay, let me call his dad; I will call you back."

"Well, where did you last see him?" I asked. "Where do you think Will could be?"

"No, no, no, Rita, listen to me," Jaime said. "Rita, he died. He's been killed."

Turns out that when the unsupervised kids at the barbecue decided to run across the street, my son didn't make it. He was hit by a car and died upon impact. The driver wasn't drunk, and he wasn't speeding. He simply couldn't avoid Will, who ran out in front of his car. I was in disbelief. I dropped the phone, my mind was raging, and my body began to shake violently. It felt like I had been left alone, naked, in the snow. All my fears about my ex-husband being an unfit father were confirmed at that moment, and I hated him.

At the thud of the phone hitting the floor, my best friend said, "What's going on?"

Emotionless and blank, I told her, "My son is dead."

Lifelessly walking into the bathroom, I turned on the shower and ran the water as hot as the knob would allow. I stripped off all my clothes and let the water run down on me for what seemed like hours. I couldn't escape the pain. If there had been an ocean, I would have dove into it. I likely would have drowned myself. Although water can be very healing, the pain was too intense.

When I got out of the shower, I took my new black outfit out of the shopping bag, packed it in a suitcase, and booked my flight. I traveled alone, refusing every one of my friends and family members' offers to go with me. When I boarded the plane, I was still in a state of shock, numb to everything around me. It was as if I'd been watching a movie or a play, and I'd merely been a member of the audience and not a participant. As I sat waiting for the plane to take off, I saw a mother breastfeeding her baby, a high-school girls' soccer team laughing, and an elderly couple helping each other settle. I felt like time stood still, but all these lives continued around me.

Only I knew my pain. I had never felt so isolated and invisible to those around me. I sat in my seat sobbing, afraid of what I would encounter when I landed; I wanted to die. My sister-in-law picked me up from the airport. "I am so sorry," was all she could say, and I had no response.

When we got to my ex-husband's house, I had an out-of-body experience; I wanted to grab him by his neck and squeeze it until he dropped. I wanted to scream into his ears, "GROW UP! GROW UP! GROW UP!" with a megaphone shattering his eardrum. Instead, I went directly to my son's room, crawled into his bed, and cried into his pillow.

Slowly checking the room, I noticed his slippers placed neatly next to his Pjs [He'd always set his night clothes out for easy access before bed], there was a box with various rocks, and his suitcase sat by the closet door. He probably had it out preparing for his return home. I walked over to the suitcase to see my son's things and to hold a part of him. I opened the suitcase, picked up one of his shirts, and clenched it tightly to my chest. As I looked down, I noticed an envelope. Though William was supposed to come back home in seven days, he'd written me a letter that he hadn't yet sent.

I opened it, "I love you," it read, "and I hope you like this CD that I got for you." My heart melted as I envisioned the words coming from the voice of my sweet nine-year-old. I still keep that letter and CD beside my bed as a reminder of my son's huge heart and boundless love.

I stayed in William's room the whole night without speaking to anyone. My ex nor his sister dared to try to cross me. The next day, my mom and aunt arrived; I felt safe to come out. I found my strength, and together, we went to the mortuary to view Will's body. All I remember thinking was that my son had very long eyelashes. They were enviable, and everyone commented on them. His head was crushed, and I remember looking at him and thinking, "Thank God he's got his eyelashes." On the day of his memorial service, I kept looking at his eyelashes. They looked like butterfly wings, the intricate detail beautiful and free.

When I returned home, my friends and family offered their support, but nothing seemed to help. Two weeks later, when I cleaned Will's room and gave his things to another nine-year-old in our community, I collapsed on the floor. I look back now, and I am not sure how I survived.

One day, a few weeks after the accident, my cousin Levren visited. I was still overwhelmed and deeply sad. "You can stay where you are, which is painful," he said, "or you can get up and do something meaningful with what's happened to you. I'm here for you either way." My cousin wasn't judging me. He was simply stating what he saw to be the truth. It was my turning point. Forcing myself to get out of bed each morning, I reflected on my cousin's words. Little by little, I would wake up, cry, pray, and get out of bed. I would think about those beautiful butterfly lashes, and for a brief moment, there might have been a crease in my mouth resembling a half smile.

Three months later, I went to my first support group, Compassionate Friends for Parents Coping with the Death of Children. I also bought an Eric Clapton CD and listened to the song "Tears in Heaven" repeatedly [The song was written about the death of the artist's four-year-old son]; it made me feel like I wasn't alone. My faith in God, the power within me, the God within me, and the power of prayer my mom taught me at an early age helped me eat and take showers. Even at my lowest point, it was my prayer, my higher power, and my belief that pulled me through.

I still had faith in the sunshine. Every day, I told myself, "You can do this." If I couldn't convince myself, I'd play music or utilize non-traditional Western rituals/therapy of healing. Instead, I'd listen to Djembe drumming, known for its Indigenous practice of releasing trauma, and take yoga and dance classes; I would journal and meditate. I often asked myself, if I had died before Will, what would I want him to do? My answer, of course, was I would not want my son to self-destruct. In a way, William is the reason I am alive.

After two years, I realized it was time to figure out how to channel my pain. I decided to heal myself by helping other people manage their grief, too. I knew I needed to be proactive, and this kept me going. The old cliché says that time heals, but it's not true. It's what you do with your time that heals you. I enrolled at California State University and studied death, dying, and grief in various cultures. I became a madwoman, obsessed with spending days in classrooms and evenings in the library. I read everything I could get my hands on. I was especially captivated by what I learned about denial. I started to lead support groups and began talking to people about their grief. In doing this, I began living again.

In my support groups, I try to help people realize that they have the right to grieve and that it's natural to feel annoyed by certain questions or insinuations. For example, the most frustrating thing someone could ask a grieving person is, "How long has it been?" This question implies that they are hoping to attach a timeline to your grief. But it's not theirs; it's yours. Society tries to dictate how many days or years we're allowed to manage something. But grieving has no timeline, no agenda; it has nothing but time on its hands, unabashedly so. And the longer you grieve, the more people expect you to behave in a certain way. The whole equation feels unfair, especially when friends or family tell you, "Okay, it's been a year..." or "She was eighty-two. She lived a good life," As if that erases your sadness or helps you stop missing someone. It's a system of grieving that we learn in an invisible classroom called life, and it's inaccurate and flawed.

Through my experience, research, and work, I've learned that people don't know what to say to a grieving person. Acquaintances often assumed my thoughts and would say, "You only had one son, you poor thing," like that was a consolation. What they didn't know was that I chose to have one child, and I wanted him to be a boy. I also know people talk about me behind my back. I've heard their words. Knowing they're simply without words has helped me handle people's reactions. When others don't know how to deal with someone grieving, I suggest they simply ask the griever what they need.

Admit you don't know what to do or say. Make no assumptions. Say, "I want to be here for you. If you want to talk about your son or your daughter, I'll listen." Offer yourself. Give the gift of a book or a journal. Sometimes, it's not the words but the actions of people that help us -- a friendly keychain or kind notes, periodically. A friend sent me a card and a book on William's tenth birthday that said, "I found this little book and thought about you. You're never alone. Call me anytime." I will always remember that. The following year, she sent a card with a daily meditation book.

Surprisingly, years after my son's death, my ex-husband said to me, "You're right, and I was wrong. I have been an irresponsible and selfish person. It is my fault that our baby is gone, and I will have to live with that guilt for the rest of my life. Your anger is anger I feel toward myself. Every day and night, I think about that one decision I made."

He asked me to forgive him, and I did. It took me a while, but I did. In my heart, I know my son would want me to. He loved his father, and for that reason alone, I had to forgive him. I could almost hear William's voice as I came closer to that place in my heart. "Mom," he'd say, with those beautiful brown *eyes* framed by those memorable lashes, "love my daddy." Forgiveness was important to him.

Is waking up each day and moving on with my life, knowing that I will never see my son again, still hard? *YES*. Do I still want to give up on life? *NO*. However, there are constant reminders. Every September, when school starts, I pass kids in the playground, and it's tough for me to watch all the children laughing, playing, and running around. Sometimes, I go out of my way to avoid them. I've learned ways to manage my grief, but it doesn't subtract from what I felt and still feel for my son. I also believe that life does not end; the body just does a disappearing act. The essence, his soul, his being, and our memories are the things that stay. To all those who grieve, know, and understand that time does heal wounds, **but** it's your faith and inner strength that heal your life.

Reflection

Should there be closure after the loss of a loved one? What would closure look like specifically for you?

Do guilt, fear, and regret surface when thinking about the loss?

An Affirmative Prayer

No matter the type of loss or grief, I am reminded that I have a choice. I choose what works best for me. I choose to connect with others for support. I choose to communicate my feelings openly. I will not hide my grief, as I did not hide my love.

Repeat the following scriptures daily as a reminder of God's promises.

Just Write

Nikki Blakely-Simmons

Nikki Blakely-Simmons is a licensed **Georgia REALTOR®, Instructional Designer, Brand Strategist & Professional Development Coach, and Professional Speaker**. Her company, NBS Real Estate Group, has two foundational principles: 1) to educate, guide, and support as many people as possible in the home buying, selling, and investing process, and 2) to teach the importance of using Real Estate as a vehicle to create generational wealth.

As a multi-million dollar-producing Real Estate Advisor with certifications as a Luxury Home Marketing Specialist (CLHMS), Relocation Specialist, National Commercial Real Estate Advisor (NCREA), and Real Estate Mentor, Nikki aspires to change and transform lives through education on generating, duplicating, and maintaining wealth through buying, selling, and investing in Real Estate.

With a strong track record in building thriving teams, coaching, and training business professionals, Nikki also has a team of **78 Real Estate Agents within her Wealthy Mixologists organization** that she coaches and trains. She also owns the **Agent Wealth Builders Academy,** a Branding, Marketing, and Professional Development Coaching business assisting REALTORS® and Real Estate Agents with identifying their brand voice and identity, creating identifiable brands, attracting ideal Clientele, and creating thriving businesses.

Nikki sits on **EXP's Georgia Agent Advisory Committee as Chai,** serving as the direct liaison between EXP's leadership and its 4,000+ agents, ensuring every agent's voice is heard. Nikki also serves on the **Union City Development Authority (UCDA) as Commissioner,** working closely with City Officials and constituents on real estate matters that impact the growth and sustainability of the city.

Her accolades include being recognized as a **Top 10% Realtor,** a **Phenomenal Woman awardee by Millennium Business Advisors**, a **Woman of Achievement nominee by ACHI Magazine Awards**, a **Founder's Rising Star nominee for the RICE Awards**, a **Women Uplifted honoree**, as well as being featured in several local Atlanta magazines.

Accepting The Assignment

Nikki Blakely-Simmons

"Trust in the Lord with all thine heart; and lean not unto thine own understanding. In all your ways acknowledge him, and he will direct thy paths."

PROVERBS 3:5-6 (NKJV)

Accepting God's assignment for our lives can be scary because when we can't see what God wants us to do, be, or experience, it makes us nervous and prevents us from taking that first step. Oftentimes, the assignment is not clear because we try to create our own assignments. That is where we go wrong. God has a purpose for everyone's life, but that purpose begins with His assignment for us and not our self-assignments. When I came to this understanding, I was able to accept and walk in the assignment that God had purposed for my life. As I walk you through this journey of me accepting the assignment from God, I ask that you open your mind, your heart, and your spirit to receive the wisdom that is the foundation of me living God's assignment on my life.

We all have dilemmas in our lives. Should I stay or should I go? Should I buy this or not? Should I end this relationship or stay in it? Should I move, or should I stay put? Should I write this book or not? The dilemma in my life was *should I focus on me,* or *should I focus on the people around me.* You know, people like my family, my friends, my colleagues. You see, I was raised to care for others and taught to have a loving and empathetic spirit towards people. This, I believe, was the beginning of creating the habit of putting others before me. In the most extreme practice of that habit, I was not positioning myself to hear clearly from God.

One day, I woke up, and I asked myself, "Nikki, why are you doing what you do? Why do you give so much of yourself to others but neglect your own desires and self-sabotage your goals?" It was like a light bulb went off. I don't know where it came from, but from out of nowhere, the answer was downloaded into my spirit. What I was challenged with in that moment of self-reflection was this – now is your time to move, shift, and receive. It wasn't long before I realized that charge was the Holy Spirit telling me it was time to pivot and focus on God first, then myself. God really began speaking to me through His Holy Spirit. One of the things that He instructed me to do was create a prayer space where I could spend intimate time with Him and allow Him to speak to me, lead me, and guide me on His divine will and purpose for my life. Obediently, I turned one of my secondary bedroom closets into my war room. Daily, I began to spend time with the Lord in our intimate space, and He began revealing great and mighty things. As I began to encounter God intimately, my spiritual mindset became clearer. I then understood that before God would allow me to walk into my new assignment, I had to walk in obedience. 1 Samuel 15:22 (NKJV) says, "Behold, to obey is better than sacrifice."

God had an assignment for me; however, for me to walk in it, I had to turn my complete focus to Him and not put any person or anything before Him.

From that point forward, my prayer life and connection with God changed. I would wake every day at 5:30 am, go into my prayer closet to meditate, and listen for God's still, sweet, small voice. God didn't speak immediately; it took months of me being consistent and obedient, staying rooted in my prayer closet and close to God's Word. Frustration, adversity, and overwhelm befell me as I waited to hear from The Lord. There was conflict in my marriage; I was overworked and underpaid on my job; my daughter was going through critical life challenges. It seemed the more I was obedient – the more the enemy was attacking me.

For the next several months, I encountered increasing frustrations at my job, the arguments at home with my husband got worse, and my relationship with my daughter was strained. I asked God, "Why am I going through all of this when I am only doing what you asked of me, which was to be obedient?"

God answered, "I told you to take your focus off the things of this world and place your entire focus on me." From that point forward, I started to pray about my release from Corporate America, and I gave my marriage and daughter over to God. I finally gave all things of this world that I had no control over to God and placed my total focus on Him. In my prayer closet, I would ask God to reveal His will for my life, and I requested that He bless me with the desires of my heart. God's Word says in Psalms 37:4 (NKJV), "Delight yourself also in the Lord, and he shall give you the desires of your heart." Once I completely surrendered to the Lord, put Him first, and delighted myself fully in His Word, He revealed my new assignment, which was to impact the lives of others through speaking, coaching, and training. He revealed that I would speak on stages in front of thousands of people, saving, changing, and transforming lives while glorifying Him through my skill sets, talents, and treasures. After this revelation, I didn't know how this prophecy from God would play out; I knew my desire was peace in my home, healing, and deliverance for my daughter, time freedom, financial freedom, and the ability to use my gifts, skills, and talents in the world of entrepreneurship and business ownership.

In August of 2018, God spoke to me clearly and said it was time to leave Corporate America. You see, I was obedient; I didn't walk away before God gave me permission to, and I didn't walk away until my husband, my life partner, agreed with me. All the prayers, all the nights that I extended my hand out towards my husband speaking over what I wanted, it all came to pass. What I discovered, and what I learned in that experience, was that if I ask God for what I want, He will clearly direct my path. What I also learned in that season of my life was to truly trust and have faith in God. The Word says in Hebrews 11:1 (NKJV), "Now faith is the substance of things hoped for, the evidence of things not seen." I could not see it at the time, but I felt like the world was against me because what I wanted to manifest did not happen in my timing. It felt as if I was being spiritually attacked in the Earth realm. Little did I know, God was simply strengthening my faith in Him, girding up His Word inside of me, and teaching me to trust in His promises, His laws, and His true and Living Word.

By the end of August 2018, I retired from Corporate America. It was one of the happiest days of my life; there was no fear, no anxiety. There was nothing but peace, and I knew without any doubt that I was doing the right thing because God ordered my steps. One of my prayers had been answered, and I was so ecstatic that God had heard them. However, during the first year and a half of entrepreneurship, I experienced the heaviest trials of my life. My husband and I were going through heavier challenges in our marriage, my daughter was still going through her personal challenges, and it seemed like everything was going wrong during the time when I should have been the happiest because I manifested my goal of entrepreneurship. My REALTOR® business struggled the first 18 months, and I started to question whether I made the right decision and if I was built for entrepreneurship. The atmosphere was so heavy in my home that I could not focus on my business. Then Holy Spirit spoke to me one day, and the words I heard clearly were "super-hyper focused." This instruction from God took me back to the time when He initially told me to create my prayer closet to establish an intimate relationship with Him. God was telling me, once again, to make Him the center of my focus. I took that revelation and immediately acted. I got "super-hyper focused" on God and the business He blessed me with, leaving all my cares and worries to Him so that I could walk successfully in His divine will and purpose for my life. It was during this season I learned that when trials and tribulations constantly befall us and warfare is all around us, it's because God is preparing us for a breakthrough and a blessing.

As the months went by, I committed myself completely to being obedient to God's instruction. I created a daily schedule, which I followed without fail every day for six months straight. I became committed to the vision that God had given me, and I did not allow anyone or anything to impede me from manifesting God's vision for my life. In God's perfect timing, the arguments ceased in my home, my daughter was delivered and healed from her challenges, and my real estate business became a great success. In my second year of being an entrepreneur, I became a top producing agent in Metro Atlanta, receiving numerous awards, building a team of over 70 agents, serving as Co-Chair of the Georgia Agent Advisory Council for my Brokerage, as well as Commissioner of the Union City Development Authority. Being obedient to God positioned me to get clear on and accept my assignment. It also positioned me to be abundantly blessed so that I could be a blessing to others.

Sacrifice is when we decide what we want to do; obedience is when we do what God wants us to do. My absolute favorite scripture in the Bible is Proverbs 3: 5-6 (NKJV), "Trust in the Lord with all thine heart; and lean not unto thine own understanding. In all your ways acknowledge him, and he will direct thy paths." Listen to God and allow Him to be the light unto your path and the lamp into your feet. Get super hyper-focused on God and understand the power of putting Him first and yourself second before all things. When we do this, we begin to live a life of Godly prioritization; we live the life that God has purposed us to live, and we can then say we have accepted the assignment. As you matriculate through this thing called life, pray to have a discerning spirit, listen to God, create the intimacy with Him that He desires, and watch Him move you into His divine life assignment.

Reflection Question

What steps should you take daily to quiet the noise and hear God's still, sweet, small voice as He's moving you and guiding you to your divine life assignment?

An Affirmative Prayer

The Lord says that I can do all things through Christ who strengthens me. I affirm that today and every day moving forward, I will put God first, creating an intimate relationship with Him. I trust Him wholeheartedly to guide me into my divine life assignment. Amen.

Just Write

Lakisha Moore

Lakisha Moore is a multifaceted individual with a diverse range of skills and passions. Alongside being a wife and mother to three adult children and five grandchildren, she is an accomplished administrator, teacher, entrepreneur, and creative. Lakisha is happily married to Jason Moore, who serves as the lead Pastor of Gathering on The Rock Church, and she works with him as the Director of Operations.

Her personal interests include spending quality time with her family, exploring the outdoors, traveling, and expressing her creativity. Lakisha is deeply committed to empowering and encouraging others, and she does so through various avenues such as mentoring, coaching, public speaking, preaching, teaching, and writing.

Professionally, Lakisha started as a licensed cosmetologist and owned a six-suite salon. After a long stint in the health and beauty industry, she embarked on a new journey and went back to school to become a neurosurgeon. Following her Bachelor of Science degree in Neuroscience and a minor in Psychology, Lakisha pivoted her career to education and became a teacher. She furthered her education by earning a Master's in Education Administration and is currently serving as an assistant principal at an elementary school.

The Least of Them

Lakisha Moore

1 Samuel 16:7 (NIV) But the L ORD said to Samuel, "Don't judge by his appearance or height, for I have rejected him. The LORD doesn't see things the way you see them. People judge by outward appearance, but the LORD looks at the heart."

JOSEPH, PAUL, DAVID, RAHAB, DEBORAH, QUEEN ESTHER, MARY MAGDALENE

"I'll be back, but not as an inmate!" I remember the day I was released from county jail like it was yesterday. Those two months of lock-up and being away from my kids seemed like two years. Sadly, with their mom imprisoned, they were separated. My four-year-old son was with my mom, and my three-year-old daughter was with her dad. During one visit, my son cried and said, "I hate the police!" I didn't want him feeling that way and made sure that was his last visit. I was jailed for the bad choices I made. The police were doing their job. Christmas, New Year's, my birthday, and Valentine's Day were all spent in lock-up.

Never in my life or wildest dreams would I have imagined being locked up. That experience changed my life. Those heavy metal doors slammed behind me, signaling that leaving was not an option, not then.

"Strip down, bend over, open your cheeks, and cough," said the guard as I stood naked in a room with another guard and several other women during intake. The humiliation, degradation, and embarrassment were all the beginning of a lifetime of regret. Once my intake was complete, I was escorted to my temporary home for the next 60 days. Upon entering, I noticed that everyone was in a white jumpsuit except for me; mine was orange.

I asked, "Why am I the only one in an orange jumpsuit?"

The guard replied, "You will run."

Her reply made sense. One of my offenses was boosting - stealing clothes - and during one of those ill-fated charades, I was caught but tried to run. If that wasn't enough, I got into a scuffle with security as I tried to flee. Unfortunately, that little scuffle landed me an upgraded conviction of robbery instead of theft. So, when an inmate like me was given an orange jumpsuit, that notified the guards that they would flee. I wanted to cry so badly, but having watched several prison movies, I knew the first piece of advice given to anyone going in was not to show weakness. Granted, I was only in the county jail, but based on stories shared with me, the county facility was just as horrifying.

My initial thought as I settled in was, "God, you hooked me up for real!"

I know my decisions landed me there, but my consequences didn't really match the crime. The ladies around me committed far more serious crimes, including murder. They were getting ready to be transferred to do life sentences. I only had 60 days; then I could go home. There was so much that transpired in that short amount of time. Things that changed the course of my life forever.

I stepped into a different world. My life changed instantly and dramatically. The environment was different. I wasn't accustomed to the constraints of where I could go and when I could go. If I wanted to leave my house at whatever time I chose, I could do that. In contrast, there was no leaving the cell once lights were out and cells were locked. The food was horrible there. We didn't have many favorable choices, so we had to make the best of what was given. On the outside, the choices were endless. One main big difference for me was I knew no one there. Who could I trust? Who could I talk to or confide in? At least on the outside, I had a select few. In there, it was a world of unknowns.

The North Tower was a maximum-security tank where inmates resided. Inside the tank was a huge open area with two rows of cells on one side that extended about halfway along the tank from left to right with top and bottom rows. It was sort of an oval-shaped space. The open area was our day room with a TV and dining area. Also, in that space were two showers covered only by make-shift curtains on a rope. Everyone in the tank had to share those two showers. Each cell housed two ladies and had a top and bottom metal bunk with a bunk mattress and a combi unit (which is a toilet, sink, and water fountain all-in-one). I don't quite remember the number of ladies that were in my tank, but we were full. The guard station was on the outside of the tank, so we were caged or entrapped with no way to escape. Our only way out was by permission. I had to embrace my temporary but new normal.

Then, there was the drama that started immediately. I quickly learned that jail was not the place to try and make friends but to survive. I was told that Big Phyllis liked me and to watch out for her. Big Phyllis was the bulldog, or bully of the tank, who got her way. Most of the ladies stayed out of her way or gave her what she wanted due to her size, stature, and bark. I really wasn't afraid of the people, but I was afraid of getting into trouble that could lengthen my time. Still, I had to let Big Phyllis know that little Kisha didn't swing that way, and she would catch that broom handle if she even attempted to come my way. Although I was only five feet one and a 150-pound shorty and Big Phyllis was a five eleven, 250-pound giant, I was not intimidated. My response to her advances informed other cliques of my stance.

After distancing myself from the drama or any women associated with Big Phyllis, I changed cells and ended up sharing one with a young lady who had just turned 17. She had made a terrible choice that would send her off for almost a lifetime. My heart hurt for her because she was also eight months pregnant. She had joined a gang of boys in her neighborhood who were doing foolish and reckless things. During the course of one of those reckless things, they killed a store owner. Although she didn't pull the trigger, everyone in the car was tried for murder. Like me, she was drawn into a world that was opposite of her upbringing. Her nature didn't align with the mess she had gotten herself into.

Crazy things kept erupting in that place. Me and my cellmate pretty much stayed in our cell away from the crazy. Although we made poor choices about who we hung out with and the things we did, you could tell we were different and didn't belong there. One of the craziest things happened with a lady named Brenda. She was placed in a cell with an addict (like Brenda) but also had mental problems. Before being arrested, Brenda wrapped dope in plastic and swallowed it, so she could poop it out when she got inside. She told some other addicts there what she had done, so they all gathered in that tiny cell and caught her poop before it hit the water to find the dope. They did it and got high off that little bit of dope.

A few days after that, the guards didn't give Brenda's cellmate her psych meds. She had a manic episode while the cells were on lock and began banging her head on the walls until she produced blood. Brenda was yelling and screaming for help, but the guards wouldn't open the cell door to let her out. Nor did they come to restrain her cellmate.

At some point, I was compelled to start reading the Bible. When the book cart came around, I grabbed a gently used Bible off the cart. I believed it was there for me. I never really took time to read the Bible at home but was drawn to it while locked up. Initially I attempted to read it from start to finish, but realized it wasn't that easy. Then, I was led to start in the book of Proverbs. My mindset started to shift. God was opening my mind and heart to something new, something that would change my life: His Word and Him. As I was exploring the Bible, I ran across some scriptures of protection. I wrote those scriptures on two sheets of paper and used toothpaste to stick the papers on our cell window. The guards never asked us to remove the papers. God made us the exception.

After placing those papers on our cell windows, no one came near it or us. We only left out to catch chow (that's to eat), shower, and get mail. At times, I'd look outside of my cell into the common areas and see restless souls pacing with no rest. Though I hadn't committed my life to Christ yet, He allowed me to see beyond what the natural eye could comprehend. God gave me a glimpse into the spiritual realm, even seeing why they wouldn't come close to our cell after posting the scriptures of protection. God was calling me; I had to take heed. There was so much more that happened during what I now call my time of revelation. During one of the lowest points in my life, God was right there with me.

It's good to have that portrait hanging in the foyer of the library in my mind. The portrait of the jail experience. The portrait of what my life could be like if I didn't change the course of my life. A life of addiction, shame, hopelessness, restlessness, and imprisonment. That portrait is a remnant to remind me of a lifestyle that I dare not revisit. A lifestyle of physical, mental, and spiritual imprisonment.

How did an honor student, uniquely talented in almost anything I put my mind and hands to do and well raised, end up in jail? It all started a little something like this...

"Kisha, let's skip school and go to the mall."

One of my childhood friends threw out the hook of deceit, lying, and stealing, and I bit. I was in high school at the time and highly influenceable; my "yes" was given a little too easily. Little did I know that one bite would cause me a lifetime of pain! Now that I think back, we didn't think those shoplifting exploits through well at all. In fact, we skipped school to go to a major department store during a time that was obvious that we should have been in school. I can't even remember how we got there. I just know we got there.

The anxiety swelled up inside of me as I entered the store, a novice, scared, and hoping I wouldn't get caught; not caught stealing, but caught skipping school. I entered the store with my drawstring duffle purse with a beeper bag inserted. The beeper bag was foil paper lined with duct tape. I made it in the shape of my duffle bag purse to fit in perfectly. I also had a small sharp pointed knife to remove certain tags that would still cause the sensors to sound an alarm. I was put into the game of retail theft and quickly trained in it by the best. My heart began to pound erratically. I was sweating and shaking and wanted to drop everything and run out of that store. It was too late; I had come too far to abort the mission.

The next thing I remember, we were at one of the girls' houses sorting through the goods. It was me, my best friend, and her friend who taught us how to boost. I couldn't believe it! I had stolen top, name-brand shirts ranging from $75 to $150. Those were clothing items that were outside of my momma's financial reach. Don't get me wrong, Momma took good care of me. I had nice clothing, but not the brands that were popular at that time. Definitely not the brands teens desired then. After we kept what we wanted, we took a trip to several beauty salons to sell the rest. Not only did I come up with nice clothing, but I also made money too! I was sold; that was the beginning of my imprisonment-mentally, spiritually, and physically.

Momma never noticed the clothing that I obtained from stealing. I made them unnoticeable to her. Not long after that introduction to a world of sin came another temptation, then another. After a while, I couldn't keep the lifestyle I had slipped into from Momma. She knew something was different about her little girl. I was slipping away from her and into a dark world of the unknown.

A wise woman once told me that sin comes in pairs. That was an understatement in my case. Sin targeted me and came in droves, one after another. To be spiritually accurate about what took place in my life at such a young age, the enemy of my earthly assignment dispatched some of his strongest warriors upon me one by one and back-to-back.

First, it was the bait of thieving, then men, then drugs. I was on the verge of dropping out of high school. Life took me fast and quickly. I began rebelling against my mom and her house-hold rules. Soon after the rebellion showed up, I left home. I knew I had to. I wanted to do what I wanted to do, but I didn't want to keep disrespecting my mother. Something got a hold of me and blinded me. That is what a life in darkness does, it keeps us from thinking in truth, light, and love. I moved from my mom's house into my boyfriend's mom's house, then into an apartment with the friend who introduced me to stealing. I was too far gone, mentally, spiritually, and physically. My friend and I both were sinking deeper into a life that could have sent us to jail for life or the grave. The most astounding part to many who hear our testimony is that we were seniors in high school living like this. Most could imagine young adults venturing into the type of lifestyle we had ventured into, but not teenagers still in high school. To top off our spiraling out of control, we both found out that we were pregnant, one month apart! There we were, pregnant, hustling to pay our bills, and on the verge of dropping out of school. I know God was with us because we survived and were kept even in all of our craziness. As a matter of fact, our high school principal told our counselors to change our schedules so that we only had to attend the classes needed to graduate and then go home.

I eventually graduated. I wobbled my eight-month-pregnant self across that stage and claimed my diploma! I was proud of myself for once, and for real. I didn't steal that; I didn't sell drugs to get it or sleep with any man. At that time, I was in hustle-to-survive mode, trying to make it by any means necessary. However, I wasn't out of the deep ditch I dug for myself. I didn't have a job and was doing what I had to do to survive. I didn't realize then that the reason so many ill-fated opportunities presented themselves to me was because of the great calling upon my life.

Those were ill-fated opportunities that could have brought about the death of what God created me to do and the people I was destined to impact. As I pointed out earlier, the temptations came in droves, and I accepted almost every one of them that came my way. It was all piling up and catching up with me. I was tired and started realizing that my life was going in circles. The life I was living was going to be the death of me. I didn't know how to change or get out.

God had an experience stored up for me, one aligned with the path I chose, that would open my eyes and be the beginning of a way of escape. Even though it was a chastising experience, God kept me. I know without any doubt that those 60 days in the county jail was an experience specifically crafted by God to sit me down and get my attention. While I was there, I was shut away from everyone and everything that kept my attention- men, drugs, hustling, money. None of that mattered to me during that time. I just wanted to be free again. I wanted to be free to be with my kids and start my life over. By the time my enlightenment was happening, I was two kids deep with no sleep. I desired a better life for me and my kids. Lord, I just wanted a second chance.

Paul's Conversion- Acts 9 (NIV): 13 "Lord," Ananias answered, "I have heard many reports about this man and all the harm he has done to your holy people in Jerusalem. **14** And he has come here with authority from the chief priests to arrest all who call on your name."

15 But the Lord said to Ananias, "Go! This man is my chosen instrument to proclaim my name to the Gentiles and their kings and to the people of Israel. **16** I will show him how much he must suffer for my name."

Like Paul, God had to open my eyes and set me apart from the people and places of my normal places and routines and put me in an unfamiliar place: jail. He knew He could draw my attention in jail. God spoke to me, a sinner. Reading the Bible while locked up was all I had; it was a comforting experience. I learned so much. My mind was being renewed and my heart transformed to see life as it should have been from the beginning. Through reading the Word of God, I was tapping into a side of me that I knew nothing of. From that moment forward, I decided to live better and do better, starting where I was.

Paul's prayer for spiritual insight- Ephesians 1 (CSB): 18
I pray that the eyes of your heart may be enlightened so that you may know what is the hope of his calling, what is the wealth of his glorious inheritance in the saints,

Reflection

I really don't know if I could have avoided circumstances in my life. I know that they shaped my testimonies and put me on a course toward the purpose of my creation. One thing I know for sure is that it was, and is, all for God's glory! He has chosen "the least of them" to carry out His plans. How else can I boast that I am now an educational leader in an independent school district with such a rocky background? But God! It also is not lost on me that He placed me at a middle school, nurturing the age group where my choices started leading me down a dark path, an age where kids are highly influenceable and delicate. Middle school is an age where Satan, the enemy of our souls, loves to employ his playground antics. I am on assignment as one who has overcome and one who comes to set the captives free. How else can I boast that God has restored all that the cankerworm (Satan) has eaten up? He has tried to destroy any hope I had in life. I am remarried to the love of my life (the first marriage was post-lock-up and an entirely different and inspiring testimony), someone with a similar past as I, one who comes in the name of Jesus and walks in all boldness of Christ. Together, we have formed a prison ministry that is impactful and known throughout the State of Texas and beyond. Together, we lead a group of Christians who are solid as a rock and help us carry out God's Kingdom Agenda! My husband and I are blessed. My kids are blessed. The fruit of our vine prospers and fails not. God has indeed strengthened this weak soul of mine and turned my sorrows into joy. For that, I am forever grateful.

There was and is so much more to my story that can't be encapsulated here. My life, my story, and this book in which I am entrapped is a compilation of victories that are individually important and effective to various readers. While I cannot comprehensively tell the story here, my hope is that this fragment of my story encourages the reader to have hope. Whether you are or were the thief, victim of enticement or enticer, harlot, dropout, drug dealer, or whatever sin beholds you, there is hope. My hope in sharing my story is that someone views this as a leaf of hope to rise above their circumstances and tap into God. Nothing is too hard for God to deliver us from. He is The Creator of all things, so we should consult Him in all things. Rise above the embarrassment, the pain and shame, the depression and insecurities, or anything that attempts to hold you back from walking in a life of prosperity as God has intended.

I am thankful for all God has done. He has given me beauty for ashes, and I rejoice in it. I boast not for my own glory but for Christ and my story that was written by the hands of God. Victory is my ending! What is your story? What will your ending be? Join me on this journey with Christ so that together, we can celebrate your victory. For God will choose the least of them to accomplish His plans and expound His glory!

Affirming Prayer

Dear Heavenly and most precious Father. I come to You with a thankful heart. Lord, I ask and pray, in the name of Jesus, that Your Holy anointing be upon this works and reach the masses. I pray that it doesn't just reach the masses but makes a huge Kingdom impact. Father, I'm thankful that You are God and You are good. I'm thankful for the good and the bad, knowing that as long as I am in You and You are in me, I shall come out victorious! Lord, I ask and pray, in the name of Jesus, that You bless the reader and doer of this text. As they read, move upon their hearts to do something life changing and warranted by You, let them heed Your call. Lord, I thank You for the opportunity to rise up and share my story so that it may free others. Lord, do the impossible. It's in Jesus' name I ask and pray these things, Amen.

Cynthia Andrews

*"I am blessed to work in dual roles doing what
I love and enjoy the most."*

Cynthia Andrews was born and raised in Savannah, Georgia. She graduated from Windsor Forest High School and holds her Master of Business Administration from St. Leo University. She is the youngest of four girls and has one younger brother. At the age of 19, she moved to Atlanta, Georgia, where she continues to reside. She and her husband of 30 years have two adult children together, and she is the stepmother of two beautiful daughters and a grandmother of six.

Her career ranges from Accounts Payable/Receivables to Income Auditor. She retired from the Metropolitan Atlanta Rapid Transit Authority (MARTA) as a Pension Specialist. She has since returned to the workforce and obtained a second career with a major airline as a senior analyst in HR Operations.

Cynthia became interested in baking in 2014 after seeing a person's photo on a cake. Almost ten years later, she is a self-taught baker and the owner of Baked XPressions, where she specializes in personalized baked goods and treats. She is blessed to work in dual roles doing the things she loves and enjoys, and she is passionate about people doing what they love rather than working.

The "No" That Saved My Life

Cynthia Andrews

For I know the thoughts that I think toward you,
saith the LORD, thoughts of peace, and not of evil,
to give you an expected end.

JEREMIAH 29:11 (KJV)

Not being present in that moment saved my life. My dad followed the same routine for many nights when taking my mom to work, but this time was different. This time, Dad said, "No," when I asked to tag along.

I was eight years old, the youngest of four girls, and my mom was expecting a new baby in a few months. My mother worked the night shift as a nurse at a hospital, and my father worked for a steel company. My parents shared a car, and my father would take Mom to work at night. My older sisters attended church services regularly, and many times, I would go with them.

On that night, I was at home with my parents, watching mom preparing for her shift. She always polished her white nursing shoes, ironed her scrubs, and laid out everything she needed for work. Once she was dressed, the three of us would get into the car to drive her; we did the same that night. But for some reason, at around 10:30 p.m. my father stopped at my grandmother's house (who lived a block away) to drop me off.

I didn't understand why, so I asked, "Can I go with you?"

My father said, "No," which hurt me to my heart. I cried myself to sleep.

My sisters were on their way home from an evening church service at around 11:00 p.m. when they passed an accident involving a train and a car that looked like my parents' vehicle. Obviously, they were worried that my parents were in the accident and shared their concerns with family at my grandmother's home. My aunt was adamant that my mom was at work and my father was at home. She took my sisters to our house to show them that my father was there. Our house was dark. She then went back to her house and called the hospital to see if my mother was at work. This was the moment she found out that my mother had been involved in a car accident and was now a patient. The car they drove by was, in fact, my parents' vehicle. The train had hit the car on the driver's side, killing my father instantly. My mother, seven months pregnant, was in serious condition.

I was awakened in the middle of the night with lots of screaming and crying at my grandmother's house. I woke up and walked into the living room but was told by my aunt, who was there trying to calm everyone, to go back to bed. The following morning, I woke up, had breakfast at my grandmother's house, and went outside to play with my cousins. After a while, we walked to my aunt's house, who lived a block away. We were playing in the living room when my aunt stepped into the kitchen and made a phone call.

I remember vividly how my heart dropped when I heard her whisper, "Nobody told Cindy her daddy's dead?"

I tried to believe that was not what I heard her say. She hung up the phone and told me to go to my grandmother's house. I was a very obedient child, so I didn't question her. I returned to my grandmother's house, where one of my aunts ushered me into a bedroom. She sat next to me on the bed, held my hand, and told me, "Cindy, your daddy's dead." I didn't know what to think or what to ask. I cried as she held her arms around me and repeated, "Your daddy's dead."

When I look back on that moment, I could have asked so many questions, but I didn't know how to process the information I received. I was always so sheltered, and everything was kept from me to protect me.

My mother remained in the hospital for several weeks and was unable to attend Dad's funeral services. My father's two brothers came to help with the funeral arrangements and prepare us for the funeral services alongside my grandmother and aunts. My father's face had to be reconstructed due to the severity of the damage. His body was in a temperature-controlled casket encased in glass. I remember that during the service, someone picked me up so I could see him in his casket. I looked at him, though I was afraid to see him lying there lifeless. It seemed they held me there for a long time; all I wanted was to get down. As I looked down at his face he looked as though he was sleeping peacefully, and I thought his eyes could open at any time. It brought back memories of when he would be asleep, and we would have to be quiet so we didn't wake him. The thought completely escaped me that he would never wake up again, and this would be the last time I saw his face.

My mother was discharged from the hospital after a few weeks, and soon after, my brother was born and named after my father. He would never know his father or have the relationship with him that my sisters and I did. He recently asked me questions about our father, and I'm sure he's riddled with many more. I know he has thoughts of what life would have been like if he hadn't been killed.

If my father had not told me "No" when I wanted to go with him that night, I would not be here today. The car was so mangled there was no way I would have survived. When I was in the car with him, I would sit in the middle of the front seat next to him. There were a few times I could not go with him when he was driving my mom around. My father was such a jokester. He would slowly pull up to the bumper of the car in front of us and get just close enough to tap it. Then we would laugh so hard. It was my one-on-one time with him. He would always make me laugh, and we would stop at the candy store for treats. He would ride me on his motorcycle sometimes, and it would drive my mom crazy. She hated it when he placed me on the motorcycle. I would have so much fun with him.

As I come across people with struggles and traumas, I realize that I can see beyond that experience and move forward with a positive mindset to succeed. I have conversed with people who have experienced similar tragedies, and they have become a product of their past traumas. They have remained mentally in that place and allowed those circumstances to stagnate their growth. I am thankful that I did not let my past be my oppressor or allow losing my father so tragically to lead me to bad behaviors or a stagnant place.

My mother struggled with this loss and being left with five children to raise on her own, but her struggle made me strong.

Someone broke into our home while we slept and stole money and my mother's wedding ring. They knocked her out when she woke up during the break-in. There were several break-ins or attempts after that. If thieves invading our home was not enough, I was forced to experience vultures who came for my innocence at 12 years old. I quickly began to look down on people I used to look up to for guidance. I was so disappointed when betrayal became the norm from those my family once trusted. A child my age should have never been exposed to such treachery, victimization, and deceit. Many things that happened never reached my mother's ears. I kept them inside and prayed and talked to God often. I watched my mother as she did what she had to do to provide and care for her children.

When I was 17 years old, one of the elders in my church grew extremely ill and was hospitalized. He had a daughter that shared the same name as me. I was contacted by a church member and told he wanted to see me. They thought he was asking for his daughter, but he wanted to see me. I went to the hospital a few days later, and when I went into his room, he did not have many words at all. He looked at me and nodded his head as if he were giving approval and smiled. I smiled back and sat with him for a short time. Although we did not speak about anything in particular, I felt as though he was telling me I was going to be okay. The unspoken words spoke volumes. He never went home from the hospital and died a short time later.

I moved to Atlanta at 18 years old. I was very trusting and found myself being taken advantage of repeatedly. They were tough experiences, but I learned so much about human nature and myself. I lost a lot by trusting people, but it did not change me as a person. When I had children of my own, I was reminded of how my mom would prepare hot meals for us every day, work multiple jobs to give us everything we needed, and never complain. My mother even went back to school to become a registered nurse while continuing to work. I tried to do the same for my children. In retrospect, I also obtained my BA and MBA later in my adult life while I worked full-time. Despite the challenges I experienced in my childhood and the exposure to things I was too young to see, I refused to allow those experiences to shape my future. I taught my children to be responsible young adults and talked to them often about how to navigate through adversities.

Embrace the struggles you experience because they are the roadmap to your future success. When you find yourself in the midst of a struggle or when you come across adversities, keep in mind that these are not struggles to break you but lessons and tests to build upon and give wisdom. See obstacles as the opportunity to show your strength, endurance, tenacity, and faith. Keep moving, and don't be paralyzed by your past. God will never put more on us than we can bear. I have learned to live by this and know that whatever is happening in my life is in His divine plan. Walk in faith and affirm your life daily.

I could only imagine the direction my life would have taken if my father were not killed. Although I could not have asked for a better outcome, and I am grateful for my life today, I probably would not have moved to Atlanta.

This experience taught me that even the simplest "No" can be the most life-changing action and prophetic warning. Learn to accept the No's and see them as God redirecting you to a greater path. You may not understand the rejection at the time, but it is truly a redirection. The "No" that saved my life allowed me the opportunity to be here today. That "No" allowed me to be a wonderful wife, stepmother to two beautiful girls and bring two beautiful children into this world. That "No" allowed me to be here to bring my mother into my home and care for her as she struggles with Alzheimer's. That "No" allowed me to be a blessing to so many others throughout my life. The struggles brought me wisdom that could only be gained by going through the trials. Let the "No" be a blessing.

Affirming Words

Our dear Heavenly Father, I ask You to bless each and every person reading this testimony. I pray that You will sustain them through the challenges they face in this life and show them the strength You already have instilled in them. Remind them that all power is in Your hands, and they should be strong and have faith. Remind them that man's "No" is a redirection, a safety zone, and a blessing. Accept the "No." Amen.

Dr. Kerry-Ann Zamore-Byrd

Dr. Kerry-Ann Zamore is a versatile individual with a diverse background as a University Professor, Licensed Clinical Social Worker, Playwright, Award-Winning Filmmaker, Author, Director, Screenwriter, and International Speaker. She is the visionary founder of KZamore Enterprises LLC and The Zamore Foundation 501c3, passionately committed to utilizing various artistic mediums to raise awareness of social issues and empower communities through education.

With degrees from the University of Maryland (B.S. in Psychology) and the University of Southern California (M.S. and Ph.D. in Social Work), Dr. Kerry-Ann brings a wealth of experience in working with diverse populations. Certified as a personal life coach, she facilitates meaningful conversations about race, gender, and social inequities.

Dr. Kerry-Ann's creative portfolio includes over 20 original stage plays and an award-winning feature film titled "Shattered Pieces." She is a sought-after speaker on Domestic Violence Awareness and Child Abuse Prevention, with insights shared at national conferences, including The Light Of Hope Conference in Alaska and The National Association of Social Workers Conference.

Committed to community service, Dr. Kerry-Ann has served on public boards and commissions, including as the Regional Representative Social Worker for the Western Region and the National Chair of the Social Work Elections Committee. She is also active in social organizations, holding leadership positions in Jack and Jill of America Inc., Links Inc., and Alpha Kappa Alpha Sorority Inc.

In her spare time, Dr. Kerry-Ann enjoys traveling and spending quality moments with her husband and 7-year-old son, who is a newly published author and entrepreneur.

Finding Purpose

Dr. Kerry-Ann Zamore-Byrd

For I know the plans I have for you," declares the Lord,
"plans to prosper you and not to harm you,
plans to give you hope and a future.

JEREMIAH 29:11, NEW INTERNATIONAL VERSION (NIV)

"...Write the Vision and make it plain..."

HABAKKUK 2:2 (KJV)

I sat at the edge of the wooden bench in a deafening silence. The long, narrow hallway was quiet; the doors were all closed. I was the only one waiting. My head hung low, and my shoulders hunched over, my eyelids drooped heavily from lack of sleep. I took a deep breath and held it in for a few seconds; I had to remind myself to exhale – exhale, please exhale. I wanted to disappear, to melt into the tiled floor like the mopped-over speckled grey and black design in the outdated flooring. I fiddled nervously with my fingernails, picking the nude paint that had begun to chip. I needed a manicure; I clasped my hands together and squeezed my palms tightly together. I could feel and hear my heart racing wildly.

I looked at my watch; it was half past the hour. It was almost time. My mind was racing; how would this end? Am I making the right decision? but most importantly, how the hell did I get here? My throat felt dry, I needed water, I needed air, I needed to run out of there. I looked at the long walkway, I hadn't noticed that people had arrived, some gathered in small groups talking. The talking was more like hushed whispers as footsteps loudly echoed in the hollow hallway. The steps tapped rhythmically in military formation; each step grew louder, closer, and fuller. I didn't look up, did not flinch. I kept my focus on the gray and black tiled floors as the footsteps grew closer. I was afraid to look up, I was too angry to look up, I was too humiliated to look up, so I focused on the tile. The footsteps stopped suddenly. My heart raced, and I could feel my heart pounding in my chest; I caught my breath and held it, my eyes still focused on the tile.

"Is this her?" I heard a crisp, curt male voice.

"Yes," a response came from another male.

Then as quickly as the footsteps had arrived, they disappeared behind wooden double doors as the sound vanished onto the plush carpet. Once again, the hushed whispers began, but I dared not look up. I exhaled quickly; tears filled my eyes, and I fluttered my eyelashes rapidly, preventing them from falling. NO, don't you dare cry here; No, not here. I focused on the tiled floor.

After what seemed to be an eternity, I heard my name; it sounded like an echo at the bottom of a pool. I listened again. It was my name; the sound jarred me back to reality. "Ma'am, they are ready for you."

I stood slowly, aware that the eyes of the whisperers were focused on me. I was nervous. My arms were wet and clammy;

I felt sweat gather at my armpits and slowly slide down my side and back. I was happy I had worn a navy-blue dress to avoid the embarrassment of perspiration stains – *never let them see you sweat* echoed in my head. The dark-colored dress hid the sweat puddles that were beginning to form under my arms. I kept my head focused on the double doors. I refused to look at the whisperers. As the door opened by unseen hands, I walked down the aisle and took my assigned seat in the witness box. I placed my hand on the Bible and swore to tell the truth. Only then did I look up. The room was filled with uniforms. Their faces were stern, suspicious, and unwelcoming. I was not one of them. I had accused one of their own, and they were angry, their eyes focused on me. I held my breath again – *Breathe, girl, breathe,* I screamed inside - until I exhaled slowly. I pressed my thumb into my palms to keep my body from shaking – I was terrified. Our eyes met for the first time in months. His nostrils flared, and his eyes were cold. He did not resemble the man that I had loved for more than twelve years. My mind unwillingly went to my college dormitory, where we met almost fourteen years prior. How the hell did I get here?

My tears threatened again, but I refused to allow them to fall. I met his cold stare and held it. He was unmoved, unemotional, and stoic. His father sat directly behind him, and his friends surrounded him. I sat in the box alone, a long way from friends and family. My parents were assigned to a military installation in the Netherlands and could not make it. My children were too young to be with me, nor would I allow it. My friends, my support, were still assigned to military installations overseas, and they were not able to fly back to be with me. We were new to this state; we had only been there for six months, too early for me to form any real relationships. I knew no one. I was completely isolated from everyone who loved and supported me. His colleagues, all in uniform, surrounded him.

"Ma'am, Ma'am," Did he ask me a question? Wait, was he talking to me? I stared into his eyes. He was a young man, maybe mid-thirties. He seemed kind, but he was in the same uniform as my husband, so no, he was not my friend. I watched his mouth move again. I remember thinking that he was talking to me. I forced my ears to listen beyond the deafening sound of my heartbeat. I blinked again and looked at his mouth. He asked, "What happened?"

My mind raced like a typhoon fueled by the ocean and wind. How could I answer the simple question of what happened? How could I discuss the years of abuse? How could I discuss the multiple times I had been slapped, punched, kicked, dragged, yelled at, and called names for simply waking up? What does he mean "what happened?" When? The last time or the first time? The time I was too late? Or the time I burnt dinner? The time the baby wouldn't go to sleep? Or the time he thought someone was flirting with me? The time he didn't like my hair or dress? Or the time I spent too much money on groceries? The time my friends came over? Or the time I didn't answer him? The time the TV was too loud? Or the time I wanted to die?

"Which time, sir? Because it happened all the damn time! This has happened since we met." I yelled.

The young man looked at me in absolute silence. He seemed stunned. The room was completely silent; I surveyed the room, and all eyes were fixed on me. I could hear the humming lights. Was that my voice? I didn't realize I had said it out loud – I didn't recognize my own voice. I had been silent for so long; I was lost in my own head for so long that my voice had become an unwelcome foreigner. I paused in shock. It was my voice, and yes, I said it aloud. I paused, I started again, but this time I slowed down. I looked at my attorney, the judge, and then at my husband - the abuser, the source of my pain – and for the first time, I gave myself permission to speak. "I don't recall a time where I was not yelled at or hit during the course of my marriage," I said. "I was always afraid to damage his military career or break up our family, and I was also just afraid of him. This time was the scariest. This time, he had a gun." I used my voice.

I testified for close to two hours. I was drenched and exhausted when I left the stand, but this time, my head was held high. I saw the uniformed faces as they nodded in my direction. Their cold and unwelcoming faces were now transformed. They acknowledged me, "Ma'am," as I passed by. I made certain to meet their eyes. I wasn't afraid anymore. Then, I saw the doors, the uniformed man standing at the door, and the paintings that I had not seen before. I passed by the whisperers in the hall; they were in suits and uniforms. I lifted my chin and walked gracefully past them towards the exit. I paused next to the American Flag - freedom. I was finally free.

Overcoming domestic violence was the moment I gave myself permission to live out loud and unapologetically become the person God destined me to be. Sharing my lived experience was how I regained my voice and eventually propelled me into purpose. But I had to do the hard work of recognizing and admitting that I had been a victim. The hardest part for me was admitting that I needed help to regain my life. I had to use my voice; the work was to release the fear and shame of my toxic relationship; it was the work of unpacking baggage that I had carried for years.

I wish I could say that after the experience of testifying, I lived out loud immediately; unfortunately, it didn't happen that way. Speaking the truth and using my voice shook the very core of who I was. Verbally expressing my years of abuse causes me to feel lost all over again. I had to go through a process of rebuilding and shedding every broken thing in me to let light in. The first step was to confront the negative thoughts I had adopted because of the verbal abuse I had taken. I had to change the way I thought about myself and my life. I had to physically say nice things about myself and affirm myself aloud to counteract the negative words I had begun to believe.

The second step was to replace those negative thoughts with words that affirmed who I wanted to be. I had to begin to walk in the newest of thoughts to manifest what I wanted to be. I began changing the way I spoke to myself and about myself, and I also had to remove people and places that did not promote my new, healthier sense of self. I had to become intentional about myself.

Weeks following the testimony, I spent days under the blankets in my dark room, sometimes unable to move past my shame, pain, and loss of the life I once had. Although it was an abusive relationship, it was a life I had become accustomed to, and living differently was an adjustment that I was uncertain about how to navigate. I awakened only to care for my children and went back into bed as soon as I dropped them off at school. Even when I spoke positive words to myself, I didn't know how to recover. I had lost almost 14 years of my life, and positive words did not achieve what I needed to move past my pain.

I remember sitting in my large walk-in closet one evening crying. I didn't want to leave the house, but I didn't want to cry anymore. I tucked my head between my legs, and I screamed. I screamed for all the years I had remained silent; I screamed for the unspoken words that were still locked in the residue of my mind, and I screamed just to hear my own voice again. I screamed until my voice became a hoarse whisper, and then I stretched my tired muscles out across the closet floor and cried. I needed help.

I felt naked, exposed, and completely alone. I was uncertain of how to make new friends as a single woman who had survived domestic violence. Although I had begun to speak differently to myself, I was still vulnerable. It didn't happen immediately; I had to be intentional and purposeful about moving differently.

"Lord, I don't want this. I need YOU, and I don't know what to do or how to begin again; please help." It was a simple prayer. But it was the beginning of something new. I had always been fearful of being alone because I was told repeatedly that without my marriage, I would be alone and destitute. To counteract those thoughts, I did something bold for me. I purchased my own home and a new vehicle. It was my first step of defiance and rejection of negative thoughts. I went on vacation with my dearest friend. I took myself out on dinner dates and to the movies. I fell madly in love with myself, but it was a process that took time and work.

I had a passion for reading and writing since I was a young child. I began to read everything again, from classical stage plays to romance novels and self-help and faith-based books. I wrote poems, short stories, and plays. Writing was cathartic; it released the voices in my head and allowed me space to breathe and think.

I went to the nearest bookstore. The intent was to find a self-help book. Instead, I picked up a pink leather women's journal. There was an encryption on the cover: *"For I know the plans I have for you," declares the Lord, "plans to prosper you and not to harm you, plans to give you hope and a future." (Jeremiah 29:11).* I smiled, for the first time in a long time, I felt a sense of peace. I took it as a sign that God was still with me and speaking to me. I purchased the journal and sat at the table at Barnes and Noble, filling in its blank pages. I wrote – "The day we met, he drove up in a red candy apple BMW; I was sitting in the window of my dorm room and thought, wow, he's gorgeous, and he is talking to me." I began to write about each phase of my marriage, and I saw the root and pattern of where I lost myself.

Each time I could see where I had lost a part of myself. I spoke life into it by writing affirmations and prayers of healing for the younger version of me. I wrote, and I cried, and I cried, and I wrote, I prayed, I sang, I laughed. Before I knew it, I was no longer writing my hurts; I was writing my purpose for living, my purpose for joy. I began to share my journaling with my therapist, and she encouraged me to keep sharing. Little did I know, she had begun the first step of propelling me to my purpose.

Purpose found me the day I used my voice to remove shame and silence. As I released my own shame, guilt, fears, rejection, and low self-esteem, I was fueled with determination to help other women who lived in the trauma and shadows of intimate partner violence. As a social worker I had the basic tools, however, I wanted to use my voice in a different way. I wanted to reach an audience that would not necessarily attend a therapy session. Five years removed from my abuse, I began to speak at large conferences to share awareness about domestic violence by sharing my story. Since I loved performing arts, writing plays became my safe space, and directing community and church theater became a growing muse. I decided to tell my story, and the story of other nameless and voiceless victims, in a play. We sold out a local theater three times. I provided safe rooms with therapists, law enforcement, advocates, and community resources for anyone who wanted support. There was an overwhelming response from the community.

My pain and shame were on stage for all to see, but this time, I wasn't ashamed or afraid - this time, I was transparently helping others become free. I wanted every person living with abuse to know that there is freedom, light, love, and laughter after abuse.

I found myself smiling and laughing a lot because I felt light. I also began to attract the attention of several community leaders, who encouraged me to share my story at conferences and workshops. I felt new energy surging through my veins. I didn't feel like a victim; I felt victorious. I partnered with a filmmaker and decided to produce my story as an educational film. I called the film *Shattered Pieces*. The pieces of my life once shattered helped me become strong. The film was previewed at film festivals worldwide and won numerous awards. It was also previewed at universities and at the military installation where my voice was birthed. I recall the day the film debuted. I sobbed. I sobbed for the girl who didn't know how God was going to use her so mightily. I sobbed because I had finally found my place in the world.

The key to finding purpose is understanding that we were all created with purpose and for purpose. It's not about our status, financial acumen, or education. Our purpose is simply the ability to live in truth, sharing our lived experiences daily. Purpose is being fully present, emotionally, mentally, and physically; and living toward set goals. Remember, purpose never dies; it may change and evolve, but it does not die. Sis, living a purposeful life requires self-love and acceptance. It all begins with forgiving yourself and giving yourself the grace to accept what you cannot change. Identify negative self-talk and change your mindset to move and operate differently. Shed the emotional and mental baggage that weighs you down. Unresolved issues and trauma stunt growth, which in turn stunt's purpose. Don't hesitate to seek professional help if you need it.

I now live my purpose using my voice to share education and awareness through performing arts. I tell my story with the central goal of giving voice to those who are silenced. I found my purpose when I used my voice on the stand. I began to live my purpose when my voice became my pen.

Reflections

1. What are some steps you can take to find your purpose?
2. What can you do to live purposefully?

Affirming Words

Yesterday was the last day that I did not believe that I am wonderfully and fearfully made. I forgive myself for not honoring who I was created to be. I give myself the grace that I so easily give others. I exhale, knowing that although I have made mistakes in life, the very breath I breathe is evidence that I am still here to try again. I believe in who God says I am. I release doubt, anger, resentment, fear of failure, fear of the unknown, fear of people's opinions, fear of not getting life right, fear of anything that is not aligned with a purpose-filled path. I am becoming a better version of me with every breath I take, I will respect the process of growth. I will not shrink or hide. I am ready to take up space; I am ready to use my voice. I am ready to be unapologetically and authentically ME. In Jesus' name, Amen.

Just Write

Royleta Foster

Royleta is a North Carolina native residing in East Orange, New Jersey, and is the mother of one son. She is the grandmother of a granddaughter and grandson, which is one of her most rewarding duties. Royleta is the middle of seven children - four sisters and two brothers. As a business owner, she is the founder and CEO of Creative Living Support Services LLC, her agency where she Educates, Exposes, and Empowers adults with autism and other intellectual disabilities to the tools needed to live their desired lives. With over 20 years of experience, she continues to positively impact the lives of those around her.

Royleta received her bachelor's degree in biology from Shaw University and later her Master's in Education from Strayer University. She is pursuing her Doctorate in Human Services and desires to help increase awareness and services for those with special needs. She is a member of the New Jersey African American Chamber of Commerce. Royleta is a two-time bestselling author with a heart to help those in need; she is a natural giver and desires to be a philanthropist.

From Special Education to Special Purpose: My Journey of Faith and Resilience

Royleta Foster

Proverbs 3:5-6 (NIV). **5** Trust in the Lord with all your heart and lean not on your own understanding; **6** in all your ways submit to him, and he will make your paths straight.

"Sticks and stones may break my bones, but words will never hurt me." That is a lie!

I was covered in blood. My shirt, head, and face were saturated in it as my body lay beneath a tree. Surprisingly, I was still coherent. I didn›t realize I was hurt.

I screamed, "Dad! Dad! Is my daddy okay?"

I tried to get up, but I couldn't move. I looked around me, and people were racing toward me, panicking and shouting, "Oh my God, call 911."

A typical routine day began the downhill spiral of my life. Running into the house after school, like every Friday, I'd pack my bag, place it at the front door, and wait for my dad to pick me up for the weekend. My parents divorced when I was seven, and it had been five years of dad time every weekend. I would spend time with my dad, grandma, and cousins. The routine was that my dad would arrive and enter the house, and my mom would give him the parameters for our visit. This time was no different, except as I made it to the front room, I overheard my mom say, "Do not drink with my baby in the car!"

I thought that was odd but didn't inquire about what she meant. He grabbed my hand, and we walked to the car. I always sat in the front seat so I could talk to my dad. We hadn't made it five minutes away from my home before my dad said, "Baby girl, I need to make a stop."

Before I could ask at whose house we were stopping or why we were stopping, he had jumped out of the car. I waited, looking around, thinking that the people in the house where we'd stopped certainly had a lot of friends. A small group of people entered the house after my dad and another small group. But they only stayed a few minutes. Finally, my dad returned, and we headed to his house.

We were approaching Paton Street, one of the steepest curved streets in the neighborhood. All the neighborhood kids would ride their bikes or skateboards down this street with their hands in the air, screaming like they were on a rollercoaster. As we entered the curve, my dad lost control of the car, overcorrected, and sent us swerving. This was no rollercoaster, but I was screaming as the wind rushed in the window. My heart was thumping in full cadence. I thought my eyes would pop out of my head as I watched several objects enter our path. Barely missing the front porch; the car clipped the corner edge of a house, causing my dad to jerk the wheel, and smash into a parked car, the side of a van, and finally, a tree. The collision with the tree sent me flying through the car's windshield.

I didn't realize I was hurt until a man from the neighborhood answered my question, "It's not your dad that's hurt; it's you. We have to get you to a hospital!"

I probably would have bled out if I waited for the ambulance. EMTs and police weren't as expeditious in getting to our side of town for emergencies. The man picked me up, put me in the backseat of his truck, and drove me to the hospital.

I had a total of 50 stitches, which ran from the middle of my forehead back to the crown of my head. Luckily, there was no brain damage. The healing process took about three months, but the aftermath and healing took nearly thirty years. It was the middle of my sixth-grade year, and waiting for the stitches to heal was a nightmare. I knew it would be bad because half my hair was shaved off for the stitches. I didn't want to look at it, so I avoided mirrors.

My mom would change the bandages, and I would ask her, "Is it better?"

She would say, "It's getting there; take a look."

After about a month, I got the courage to look in the mirror. If the Bride of Frankenstein were in sixth grade, she would have been me. The doctor's attempt to reduce the scarring with additional plastic surgery (in my opinion) only created a bigger distraction and loss of hair. I didn't look in the mirror ever again.

I was stricken with such severe headaches and sensitivity to light that I couldn't go back to school even after the stitches were healed. Homeschool wasn't offered, and when I tried to read or do any type of work, the headaches would put a halt to that. After two to three months, I would be slowly re-introduced into the school setting, one to two days a week at most. Upon my return, the treatment I received from the teachers and kids felt worse than the accident.

The morning I was to go back to school was the next time I looked in the mirror. It still looked as I remembered, with scars and bulky bandages. I cried and cried. My mom came into the room with a baseball cap. How was a cap going to help me? The rules at school clearly stated, "NO HATS IN THE BUILDING."

She said, "I've talked to the principal, and she said that you can wear the hat inside the building."

What a relief! Or so I thought. The kids would laugh and point at me, never actually saying anything but laughing. I finished the year with no friends or socializing. It wasn't until the next school year, when I entered the seventh grade [still hiding my scars under a hat] that I was placed in special education classes because I had missed so much school the previous year. The teacher was not pleased to get a new student and expressed that immediately. I can't forget her words, "I don't know why they put you in here; you will never be worth anything. People like you live in the projects, have a lot of kids, and get welfare."

What did she mean? That day, I went home and asked my mom what the teacher meant. She said, "We are poor. When you live where we do, people think that about poor people."

I was more shocked at 'being poor' [my mom did her best to ensure we had everything] than I was about the rest, but that didn't lessen the stigma. One day, the class was in line headed to lunch. We stopped in the hallway, waiting our turn to go into the cafeteria, and another teacher walked by. With a swift, forceful motion, the teacher snatched my hat off my head while shouting, "You know you are not supposed to be wearing a hat!"

The kids went wild, laughing, pointing, and making jokes. I burst into tears, dropped to the floor, and covered my head. At that moment, I was determined to prove everyone wrong. Through my tears, I shouted in my mind, *I'm not a nobody; I'll show you; I will show you all!*

I worked hard, studied every night, and mastered my classes. However, that momentum of success and feeling somewhat in control of my life was shaken and totally upended upon entering high school. That same teacher from middle school was moved to high school, and she was my teacher again. This teacher wasn't the only person who compounded my insecurities.

Insecurities that were already increasing because of a deep, dark secret I was keeping. I never told anyone that I was experiencing sexual abuse. I was fearful of what would happen to my family. The repeated abuse came at the hands of the people who were supposed to protect me. The abuse lasted periodically for two years. It finally stopped when I had gotten ill and went to the doctor, only to be asked if I had been sexually active. Frightened, I said no. The doctor told me that he would do a test that would be able to identify if that were so. I said, nervous and trembling, "NO, I have not had sex!" (He didn't do the test.) When I told my abuser about the doctor's visit, it stopped. I never told anyone or spoke of it again. I buried it deep inside.

More determined than ever, I completed high school, thanks in part to being introduced to a college prep program for inner-city kids called Upward Bound on the campus of Shaw University. We had tutorials and test preparation, were taught life skills, and made college visits. College was never a thought or goal for me, but before I knew it, I had graduated high school and completed a college application to attend Shaw University.

The college journey wasn't as perfect as I had hoped, probably because resurfacing self-esteem issues [skin color, weight, trauma] compounded my academic struggle. I kept repeating to myself words my mom would constantly have us repeat, "You are beautiful children; you can do whatever you want. Don't let your circumstances define you."

Thankfully, our Upward Bound counselors were there and available. I would reach out to them for help with my subjects and motivation to, once again, push past life's pains. They gave me strategies to help me cope when I'd have triggering moments or just felt depressed. After a few failed classes, retakes, and major changes, I made it through—the first in my family to graduate from a four-year university. I graduated with a Bachelor of Science and a minor in Special Education.

I took my first job as a special education biology teacher. In my mind, I wanted to be a better teacher for students that looked like me. In fact, I went back to my high school in full regalia to show that teacher that she was wrong about me. Lucky for her, she wasn't there; no telling what I would have said. I taught at alternative placement schools for the next ten years. I taught the students that everyone gave up on. My heart was with the underdog. I was not only their teacher but a mentor, caregiver, and confidant for many of my students. Many of the students at the alternative school were products of broken homes and substance and sexual abuse and were diagnosed with oppositional defiance disorder or schizophrenia.

Keeping contact with several of my students after they completed school, I realized that they'd be returning to the same environment or worse. Something had to change; resources were non-existent for low-income families. This sparked a desire to learn more about the mental health and substance abuse field. Because of my college degree and ten years of experience working with students from the alternative school, I was qualified to be a mental health professional. I applied and took a job with a mental health agency. I worked at the agency for five years until another dose of "you will never make it" showed up in the form of the agency shutting down. There I was, 28 years old, out of work, my car was repossessed, and I was evicted from my apartment.

I thought I had progressed through those childhood insecurities, but in that season, I felt my life crumbling apart piece by piece. I was that scared little sixth grader sobbing on the floor of the cafeteria again. I had failed, big time, and I wasn't sure how I could bounce back from this. "God, what are you doing? Why am I here?" I cried out in desperation. I thought, *is this how it is going to end for me? I can't go through one more day of this life. I'll just end this like it should have when my dad crashed the car. I will take myself out of this life's equation.*

This is how I know I hadn't gotten over my past trauma. I got in the car and drove to an area where there was an old, narrow, and winding road. There were steep ditches on both sides and no side shoulder rails. I figured if I jerked the wheel hard enough in either direction, I could flip the car off the side of the road, making it look like an accident. At least someone would benefit from the insurance money. As I reached the area where it would be a perfect mishap, my cell phone rang. I looked down at it, and it was my baby sister. She would always call me several times weekly to check on me. What if I didn't answer? I didn't want to give any clues before I ended it. I pulled over and answered the phone.

My sister asked, "What are you doing?"

I replied, "Nothing, driving to see stepdad; he's in the hospital."

She abruptly cut me off and repeated, but this time in a discerning tone, "WHAT ARE YOU DOING?!" She continued, "Something is not right. What is going on with you?"

I immediately began to sob and said, "I just want to end my life. I can't do it anymore."

She said, "Stop. Wait. I want you to talk to someone."

I thought she was trying to stall me to figure out where I was. She clicked over, and a lady joined the call.

A woman asked, "Can I pray for you?"

"Yes," I replied. During her prayer, I felt a heavy weight being lifted off me, and I gasped as if I was reaching for air.

The woman said, "I just prayed the demons of suicide to remove themselves from you. Please continue to pray, trust, and believe – and find yourself a church; you must be surrounded by believers."

I would love to say that my life was happy and blissful from that point on. We all have trials and tribulations, but I know I am here for a reason- a God purpose, and I will trust that God will lead me through. After that incident, I reached out to a friend in New Jersey and said I needed a change in my life and scenery. I moved to New Jersey and got a job working as a Master Level Behaviorist. I worked for this company for one and a half years, serving our clients and observing the business side of the company. That old, *protect the underdog* feeling began to resurface as I witnessed the owners of the company treating their clients like paychecks, not showing empathy or care, or having their best interest in mind.

God asked, "Do you trust me?"

I answered, "Yes, Lord, but I don't want to be without a job or home again."

He repeated the question, but this time, a chill went down my back as I heard in my spirit, "Trust me and move."

I went to sleep wondering what He meant by "move." I woke up about two o'clock in the morning; as my eyes adjusted to the darkness, I softly confirmed, "Yes, Lord, I get it. I trust you, and I know what I have to do."

I got out of bed and immediately constructed my resignation letter. I researched the behaviorist specialty agency industry to inquire about the qualifications for opening an agency. I filled out the application and took my last 52 dollars, registered for my business license, and applied for my EIN-employer identification number. Within a month, I was approved to open my own mental health and behavior agency. "God is faithful!" I took on my first client the next week.

Adversity may continue to plague you, but you can continue to keep it moving. God has designed each of us with his plan in mind.

Throughout this journey, I clung to the words of **Jeremiah 29:11 (NIV)**, «For I know the plans I have for you,» declares the Lord, «plans to prosper you and not to harm you, plans to give you hope and a future.» Whenever doubt crept in, I turned to the passage that reminded me of my worth and potential. It became a source of strength and affirmation.

As a doctoral candidate and the owner of a business that supports adults with intellectual and developmental disabilities, I stand as living proof that adversity can be conquered. My journey from a special education student to a woman with a special purpose is a testament to the transformative power of faith, self-affirmation, and God's faithfulness.

I want to impart this message to anyone facing adversity and naysayers: Affirm yourself daily with positive words, spend time with God, surround yourself with love and support, prioritize self-care, and diligently pursue your dreams. Remember, if I can go from special education to special purpose, so can you. God has leveled the playing field for us all. Together, we can rise above any challenge, embrace our unique purpose, and inspire others to do the same. For in the darkest moments, we often find the strength to become beacons of hope and resilience, lighting the way for others on their own journeys of transformation.

Reflection

When listening to that quiet whisper, that nagging desire, or the thing you can't seem to escape, what special purpose do you believe it is revealing from God? How many people will be impacted if you don't fulfill your purpose?

An Affirmative Prayer

Always remember that no one can do what you have been chosen by God to do. You have been specially created for a special purpose.

Jeremiah 1:5: "Before I made you in your mother's womb, I chose you. Before you were born, I set you apart for a special work.

Just Write

Rosemary D. Oglesby-Henry

Ms. Rosemary D. Oglesby-Henry is a Christian Social Entrepreneur, author, and President of The P.E.T.A.L.S. Incorporation. She is the award-winning founder/CEO of Rosemary's Babies Co., a 501(c)(3) organization dedicated to empowering teen parents to master self-leadership and leave a legacy. Having personally experienced teen parenthood, Ms. Oglesby-Henry utilized her faith, social support, and determination to overcome challenges, including establishing Youth Pregnancy and Parenthood Awareness Day in Ohio in 2019.

Driven by her late grandmother's legacy, Ms. Oglesby-Henry spearheaded the acquisition of a nearly 7,000 sq ft mansion for Rosemary's Babies Co., known as the Holloway House & Resource Center, slated to open in 2024. Her written work, including "The Rose Who Blossomed Through the Concrete: Consequence vs Choice," has garnered international acclaim. She has also been featured in the documentary short, "Worth One's Salt," addressing barriers to health equity for Black pregnant teens.

Recognized for her leadership and philanthropy, Ms. Oglesby-Henry has received over forty honors, including the Ohio Governor Accommodation, and has been named among Cincinnati Magazine's Power 100 Ones to Watch. She has shared her story and mission as a speaker and panelist globally, advocating for education, teen pregnancy, trauma, and maternal health for young parents.

With over two decades of entrepreneurial experience, Ms. Oglesby-Henry has mentored and consulted with over fifty small businesses and non-profits, significantly impacting their growth and revenue. As a mother and Grandmother-n-love, she remains committed to her life mission: to be a National Ambassador for the global advancement of parenting adolescents.

Favorite Quotes

Never allow your barriers to break you; use them for your break-through.

No one can beat you down lower than you, but no one can lift you up higher than you.

Legacy is how you live and what you leave behind.

The secret of living is giving. So, gain it all and give it all away before you leave this earth.

Endure

Rosemary D. Oglesby-Henry

Seasons were created as a promise by God. No matter the element, His love will remain constant if you choose to endure. Matthew 24:13

I drove down Reading Road, a street in the urban community of Avondale, in Cincinnati, Ohio. It is the community I once called home as a little girl. It was summer, and I could see the property ahead of me, but for the first time, the porch light was on. The property looked as though it was glowing just so, like it was waiting to welcome teen parents who would soon be walking through its doors. Tears began to pour down my face as I parked on the side of the building. I started to reminisce. It had been three years and too many seasons to count. I sighed deeply. The property is still unfinished until another two seasons, I suppose. The freshly coated house covered in gray told a story of faith, a story of kindness, and a story of promise, a promise that could only be fulfilled if I chose to endure. I smiled with a sense of peace, knowing that I had chosen the paint color "Promise" to transform the 7,000-square-foot mansion from being known as a future home for castaways and unwed mothers to a haven of hope, healing, and family. A home for God's children. A home where every fixture and room were marked with my love.

As sweat began to mix with my tears, I hummed the song "This Little Light of Mine." In that moment, I thanked God for seasons, His grace, and His mercy. I thanked God for His Raven, restoration, and resilience. I thanked my Grandmother Rose, for her strength and love.

It was 2020, and I was in the third year of managing my non-profit organization, Rosemary's Babies Co., when the COVID-19 pandemic reaped and harvested around the globe. A pestilence that upended the entire nation, altering the way many of us think about life, family, people, and business. It was a time when the government mandated everyone across the country to stay in their houses. We had to view the world from digital picture screens while we patiently waited for *Big Brother* to release us. It was during this time that I was able to see the fragility of our systems, both educational and familial. It proved what economists and commentators had accessed: a United States that was broken. The pandemic was also a sobering reminder of death and the value of difficult things over pleasant ones. (Ecclesiastes 7:2)

As unpleasant as that time was for me, the three-week lockdown that would limit our freedoms for months brought a much-needed break from the hustle of work. Since opening the doors of the non-profit in 2016, it has been all work and no rest for me. Starting any business is hard, but building a non-profit from the trenches is exhausting to its core (this is my opinion, of course). Anyway, I have always believed that when God forced me to rest, it was then that God was working in my stead. This was not the first break in my life. God will force us to create margin in our lives. In the past, these breaks, or rest periods, have come at different points, bringing forth revelations or providing the reset that I needed to deal with storms both in front of me and behind me. This time, rest came with a God shift. That's right, a God *shift*?! We don't always recognize God-shifts because they might come while we are broken, are amid chaos, or they may look like a setback, but they are instances where God is positioning us to be where we may have asked to be or where He needs us to be. These shifts can also be called divine interventions or assignments.

No matter the term used, in the Summer of 2020, this shift came, and with it came death, the passing of my Grandmother Rose, for whom I am named. I look back now and am grateful for the rest that came before this shift. I found out about my grandmother's passing on social media! Outraged and unsettled by the revelation that was unsympathetically and wrongfully announced through Facebook by a family member. I recall arriving at the nursing facility where she lived, demanding to be there until she transitioned. The nursing facility tried to deny me the right to sit by her bedside due to the COVID restrictions being in place. Being strong-willed, this was not an option; I refused to let my grandmother die alone, as so many were forced to do during the pandemic, and my aunt (I will love her forever) approved my request to stay. For two days, I sat by her bedside, holding her hand and singing her favorite song, "This Little Light of Mine." On the second night that I was there, she opened her mouth, and tears ran from her eyes that had turned the most beautiful blue I had ever seen. I thought it was my imagination because my grandma's eyes were grey. I have marked the spiritual moment as the night she was being greeted at the gates by St. Peter, and he had just affirmed her name was written in The Book of Life (Revelation 20:15). My dad would relieve me the next morning, and I would learn that she took her last breath during my fifteen-minute ride home. My grandmother lived a full 93 years of life. She taught me so much and loved me even more. My grandmother, who was a teen mother, broke generational curses, overcame obstacles, and blossomed so that I could bloom.

The loss of my grandmother, as well as the silo of being locked down and restricted by the pandemic, was overwhelming; it was exhausting. I fell into a silent depression and refused to get back to work. Exactly one month and a day after Grandma's homegoing, I began waking up at all hours of the night crying. In my dreams, I could see that moment when my grandmother's eyes turned blue; I could hear her voice whispering the words "Holloway House." Daily, the same dream and the same message. I recall finally realizing that I was not being haunted, but it was a message. God was directing me towards a new assignment. The assignment, Holloway House.

To value the difficult things over the pleasant is a trying task. I am speaking from personal experience because pre and post the experience, the last thing we want to focus on is the lesson we learned, what the trial brought, or the will it took to endure. God was calling me to build something, Holloway House. Let it be known I was terrified. Accepting God's assignment was simple, but being obedient to God's plan was a whole different level of faith. I prayed a lot for grace and mercy during this time. I still do.

Let me go back very briefly. I am the CEO and founder of a non-profit that supports teen parents in Greater Cincinnati. I opened the doors of the organization in 2016, but the goal to help teen parents started when I got pregnant at 16. Transitioning into a mother was easy compared to building a non-profit from nothing. It would take me nearly 20 years to open the doors, and now, in the midst of finding a bit of footing, God commanded me to trash our strategic plan for His plan. I did not understand until I understood. During COVID, I learned that more than 35% of the teen parents we served were the hidden homeless. The government had declared a lockdown but had not considered the population of teen parents whom I served had nowhere to go. In Greater Cincinnati, if you are under 18 and have a child, there is nowhere for your baby to go if you are homeless and ejected from your home.

These teens experienced depression, were suicidal, suffered from food shortages and domestic violence, and were forced to stay in environments that were unsafe during the pandemic. While our organization supplied gift cards and emergency rides, we did not supply shelter. In fact, there was no legislation or laws that allowed helping teen parents during those trying times. It was devastating. I recall being seventeen with my baby and housing insecure; how could this still be an issue?

The epiphany came with a force that shook my being, Holloway House. My grandmother Rose was my haven when I was pregnant as a teen. Her house on Holloway was also a safe place for many kids and youth in the community. You see, God ordered me to build a haven for his babies and teen mothers, one that offered peace, love, community, and worship, a place where they could find shelter and safety. God knew that my life and experience were a mirror image of the children I served. Until that moment, I did not realize that every job, every obstacle, and every skill that I had gained in my professional and personal life were the tools and resources I needed for this assignment. That creating Rosemary's Babies Co. wasn't enough. I *had* to lose to build. Amen.

When I decided I would accept the charge to build a shelter and resource center for teen parents, I had never raised over five figures, I was a wet-behind-the-ears CEO, and I had no experience with project development. However, I viewed myself as an emerging leader in the city with few resources and connections. With all these things stacked against me, I did know a few things to be true: when you are called, the true test is to endure. I would execute God's plan in the same way I prevailed in the face of all adversities: faith, work, pray, execute.

With the light of summer beaming on my head and sweat on my brow, I found a realtor to aid me with buying one of the city's many blighted and abandoned properties through its development authority. I assumed this process would be simpler to navigate as we were still in our infancy, and there were so many properties available that needed restoration. However, COVID brought an influx in the housing market, and the process became overly competitive. The first property I bid on, my realtor said I had on Godly goggles. Laughing now, I remember the entire yellow wood structure was falling off, and rain poured in through the kitchen. Fearful of being showered by stray bullets, I stood outside on the estranged one-way street, pleading with my contractor over the sounds of the neighbor to evaluate the beaten eyesore more carefully.

My bid was rejected. To this day, my realtor and my team are still happy about that. After that decision, I was directed to a red brick mansion that had been abandoned for more than fifteen years. I knew the property well and had driven past the massive structure for years on my way to my office, wishing, "If only." When I walked into the building, its rounded archways, grand staircase, and antique fireplace made it feel like home. I wanted that house to be our home. I had my realtor put in our bid and waited for a "yes." I smiled when she submitted our proposal, knowing that God had me and it was done. That smile would fade as it took two years for that yes to come.

Following the submission of our proposal, supporters came in waves from around the city. I found myself overwhelmed by the gracious leaders who stepped in to be advisors and advocates for our initiative to buy this mansion to help teen parents. I recall speaking in front of our city council, and they voted unanimously to fund the project. It was during this time that I also met a raven who played a vital role in our future success. This celebration was short-lived when the neighborhood learned that *we* would be their new neighbors.

Like a good neighbor, I think not. It was more like NIMBY, "not in my backyard." I had never heard that acronym, and it was only following a very heated public meeting about the acquisition of the property that someone defined the term. As a Christian social entrepreneur, there are times my morals, ethics, principles, practices, patience, and faith are challenged; however, 1 Corinthians 15:58 says, "to be steadfast and unmovable," but we are flesh, and this can be hard. I am a woman of faith, but I contend to say honestly that I straddle the line between *cussing and Christ*. During the first year, with every public encounter, the uncharted boundaries remained prevalent as the "good neighbors" tried provoking a reaction that would put me or my organization in a negative light. Undoubtedly, the assault on my competence, a woman with several degrees, being publicly shamed for not knowing what I did not know. I felt crucified and persecuted by a community that feared the unknown population of little girls looking for support. A community that feared that Holloway House would bring violence to their neighborhood, cause their home values to decline, and devalue their reputation and standing in the community. Unknowing, they were doing an excellent job ostracizing themselves. When the media asked how I felt about the attacks, my response was always the same, "disheartened."

It is so easy to lose confidence, hope, and energy when it comes to relying on man. This is why we should trust in the Lord with all our hearts and not lean on our own understanding. Acknowledging him and trusting that only the Most High can make straight paths. (Proverbs 3:5-6) Though my faith wavered in man, I understood losing faith in God was not an option. I continued my regimen - faith, work, and prayer. With frustration, year two came, and so did a partial affirmation that included a six-month term agreement that most would find unconscionable, requiring our organization to raise one million dollars in six months and for me to get business coaching (even though I have a business degree). Unknowingly, these challenges created a sense of renewal in me as a child of God because it was then that God showed me His limitless grace, mercy, and love and gave me the sense of security needed to ignite my light to continue the battle to acquire the facility. A building whose red bricks now reminded me of a bloody battlefield. Through it all, I lost so much, including myself, my marriage, and my supporters, but never ever my way.

Despite all the commotion from the neighborhood, we prevailed, but we still had so many more hurdles to jump, including raising those one million dollars in six months. As I began to execute a plan to raise the funds, God sent me His Raven. To some, His Raven can be viewed as good or evil, but spiritually, the raven is symbolic of God's role as the creator and provider of all things. God knew my strength but saw my losses. He understood that I would deplete my entire cup to fulfill His mission. He knew that silently I was praying for a helpmate on my journey, that privately, I struggled with my thoughts. God knew those I lost on my journey were there to help, but a true helpmate was there at times to lead, at times to hold me up, and at times to ensure that no weapon formed against me would prosper. I never had that, and God knew. The Raven, whose eyes were golden brown, brought energy and joy into my life. The Raven would fly above, supplying me with clarity and direction. He would also fly ahead to ensure there were no traps ahead that would harm me as I forged our victory in year two. The Raven, while I would sleep, in the middle of the battle, and in times of doubt, would whisper in my ear, "endure to the end and you will be saved. This is a season; endure to the end, Rosemary, and you will be saved."

One day, towards the end of the journey, annoyed by His Raven, I asked the Raven what it meant to endure to the end. The Raven smiled, "I have been waiting on you to ask me." The passage from Matthew 24:13 signifies that God wants us to persevere. For those who are chosen, they must be persecuted and evaluated amongst the wicked. The chosen will stand firm in even the most difficult of circumstances (like a cult calling you ignorant and incompetent). You see, those who have the grace to endure to the end are the ones who are genuinely saved by grace. Those who endure and stand firm in the faith through all seasons, despite incitement to do otherwise, are showing that they are genuine children of God. Seasons were created as a promise by God (Genesis 8:22) that no matter the element, His love will remain constant if you choose to endure (excerpt from "The Rose Who Blossomed…" Oglesby-Henry, 2022). And if you endure to the end, you will be saved (Matthew 24:*13).*

One year later, I drove down Reading Road, a Cincinnati street in the urban community of Avondale, where I once called home as a little girl. I could see the property ahead, but for the first time, the porch light was on. The property looked as though it was glowing just so, like it was waiting to welcome the many teen parents who would soon be walking through its doors. Tears began to pour down my face as I parked on the side of the building. The fresh coats of exterior gray paint covered the red that was a reminder of the battle we fought to win this property. The new color told a story of faith, a story of kindness, and a story of promise, a promise that could only be fulfilled if I chose to endure. I smiled with a sense of peace, knowing that I had chosen to endure and would keep enduring until the first teen would enter the doors.

I got out of the vehicle, and as I walked toward the entry, I thanked God for grace and His love. The Raven then whispered into my ear, "I told you if you endure to the end…" I cut the Raven off with a laugh, "yes I am so glad God saved me and he loves me."

I walked into the building heavy, preparing myself for what was next.

Reflection

Based on what you have read, what does He expect from you?

What is your reward from God?

What are some practices that you can start today to help you endure?

God promises us five things:

1. Direction & Clarity | God will guide your steps, and even though you might stumble and fall, he will hold your hand. (Psalms 37:23-24)

2. Peace: God will carry all your concerns because he cares for you. (1 Peter 5:7)

3. Security: God will always provide and supply every need according to his riches in glory Christ Jesus. (Philippians 4:19)

4. Victory: God made you, will carry you, sustains you, hears you and will rescue you. (Isaiah 46:4)

5. Joy: God has given you authority over your life to overcome all the power of the enemy so that nothing will hurt you. (Luke 10:19)

Prayer

Matthew 6:9–13, (KJV) —"Our Father which art in heaven, hallowed be thy name. Thy kingdom comes. Thy will be done on earth, as it is in heaven. Give us this day our daily bread. And forgive us our debts, as we forgive our debtors. And lead us not into temptation but deliver us from evil: For thine is the kingdom, and the power, and the glory, forever. Amen"

Just Write

Roni Talley

Roni Talley is a bestselling author of four self-help and personal development books. As an inspirational speaker and communication coach, Roni's mission is to uplift and inspire others to reach their fullest potential in life. Her approach includes practical exercises to help break through trauma from the past and discover gifts and talents that have been dormant for far too long. Her commitment to overcome child molestation, domestic violence and self-limiting beliefs is apparent with her delivery of every speech. The audience embarks on a journey from trials to triumph and is inspired to move forward with purpose. Roni demonstrates her passion for helping others break through what's holding them back from living their best life.

Roni Talley is a professional event emcee and corporate facilitator renowned for her magnetic, soulful energy that inspires audiences to connect and act.

She helps audiences get to the heart of every session at live on-stage, in-studio, hybrid, and virtual events with her laser in-the-moment focus, graceful improvisation, and contagious effervescence. Roni emphasizes critical points from speakers and themes, creating continuity, cohesion, and driving deeper audience engagement.

Drawing from years of experience as a stage and film actress, radio personality, emcee, moderator, and corporate presenter in technology, healthcare, finance, and more, Roni makes complex material conversational, improvising with humor and grace. These rich experiences add to her ability to flow with the changing variables of live events. Her clientele spans large corporations like Intuit Inc., New York Life, Rolling Out Magazine, Cheryl Polote Williamson, LLC, Soul Reborn, and Congregational Security, Inc.

Embracing the Light Within:
A Journey to Restoration

Roni Talley

After three months of dating in 2018, one man, Shannon, re-kindled my hope in marriage. It seemed unreal that amidst the darkness of my past - marked by violent, insecure, and jealous husbands - I had found someone who could help heal the scars on my wounded heart. Communication, intimacy, and loving-kindness allowed us to foster a strong and fulfilling connection.

A gripping journey often begins with a painful chapter. Mine started at the tender age of six when I experienced the depths of darkness that no innocent soul should endure. The unspeakable act of molestation shattered the innocence that lay within me, casting a shadow on my path to happiness. My mother held down two jobs to care for my brother and I as a single mother. We had two different fathers, and neither were around to help out. While my mother worked late hours, I would go to a babysitter's home after pre-kindergarten dismissed. The woman (whose name I cannot remember) would feed me dinner, then leave me to watch TV on my own until my mother came to get me after work. I would often fall asleep while I watched different shows until I was gently awakened by the soft voice and caress of my mother as she picked me up and prepared me to go home. While not the most ideal routine, it suddenly came to an abrupt halt. While in the babysitter's care one day, a man – I didn't know then, but now realize he was about 20+ years old, a friend of the babysitter's son, interrupted my sleep and took me off the couch and into the bathroom. There he removed my panties and placed me in the tub, where he penetrated my vagina and anus repeatedly with his penis. As I cried and tried to scream, this monster covered my mouth and threatened to kill me if I fought him.

You may be wondering, *where was the babysitter?* Why didn't they check on you? These were the questions I asked myself over the years as well. His assault felt like it lasted an eternity. When it was over, he wiped the tears from my face, made me put my panties back on, took me back to the couch, and left me there alone. As a child, I didn't really know what had happened; I just knew that I was in pain and terrified to utter another word. This extreme physical and mental suffering happened again the next day and could have happened over and over, but my mother noticed I was behaving strangely. I was quiet, sluggish, and withdrawn, which was a drastic shift in my vibrant personality. My mom would tell me in later years that she noticed I was walking slower than normal, as if I had urinated on myself or if my private part was irritated. After giving me a bath and trying to figure out why I was exhausted, asking to go to bed at 7 p.m. instead of nine; she noticed my bloody panties and immediately began to question me about what happened. Things moved so quickly after I revealed the truth. When she discovered what had happened, my mom called the police to our home, and then she took me to the hospital to determine if any damage was done and to hopefully collect a DNA sample. I did not return to school or the sitter. Because my mom had to work, she found an alternative, safe place for me. The next thing I recall is explaining everything that happened to me before a judge and lawyers.

It was just like you see in the movies or a docuseries - I used a doll in the courtroom to explain how the rape occurred. I would point at points on the doll to describe, in great detail, how I was violated. The attorney and judge asked me to describe the home, the man, and the bathroom where the assault happened. The judge made me feel comfortable to freely explain the events. The day I testified, there was only the judge, our attorney, my mom, and two other people there. I felt safe. My mother assured me that everything would be okay if I told the truth and gave the judge all the information that I could remember about what happened. I will never forget the look of pity in her eyes as she listened to me, but I also saw pride in her posture as she sat there. The feelings of liberty and justice still overwhelm me today. My mother was so proud of me for being so brave on the stand. Part of me felt like I was a superhero and that I had done my part to put a sick criminal behind bars.

While I was not allowed in the courtroom for most of the testimony, my mother was there for every hearing. She shared what became known during the testimony. The babysitter had one son who sold drugs and had tons of young men in and out of the house. It was one of those guys who violated me. Little did I know that this was just the beginning of a series of unimaginable events that would happen to me throughout my life. Oh, and yes, they found the man that was in question, but I did not find out until twenty years later when my mother revealed to me, in a random discussion, that the pedophile had an alibi. His girlfriend testified that he was home with her and couldn't possibly have abused me. This rapist got away with what he had done to me.

As I grew older, the world around me became a haunting reminder of the pain I had endured. At the age of eight, the unimaginable horror struck me once again, threatening to consume the flickering light within my soul. This time, it would happen at the hands of my own brother, Corey, who was 11 years old. He was a troubled kid. From a young age, Corey was in and out of group homes for boys with behavioral issues. Once, he told authorities he'd often had thoughts of hurting my mother and me. Social workers felt it best for everyone's safety that he be removed from the home. We lived in a two-bedroom apartment in the Astoria, Queens, New York housing projects. Corey and I shared a room. One night while lying in bed, Corey fondled me and forced his penis in my mouth. I fought and cried and repeatedly asked him to stop. I kept saying, "I am your sister. I am your sister." Finally, after a few minutes of pleading with him to stop, he fell to the floor in shame and embarrassment. He left the room.

I didn't see him the same for many years. I didn't tell my mother for fear that my brother would get in trouble and be sent to another group home far from the family again. So, I kept this a secret for years. Can you imagine the confusion in my eight-year-old mind? The first time it occurred, it was a stranger; this time, my own flesh and blood violated me. I trusted him until that day. I always wanted to play with him, and I expected him to protect me. Yet after the sexual encounter, I didn't feel safe alone with him anymore. Comfort moved to discomfort. A natural brother-sister relationship transformed into an uncomfortable web in which I was trapped. I slept in my mother's bed from then on. Somewhere along life's journey, I believed this behavior must be normal for men. I felt powerless.

My father was absent between the ages of three and nine years old. He later explained his distance and inconsistency was due to his ego and addictive drug use. We've grown closer in my older years because I longed to connect with him and understand the dynamics of a father-daughter bond. Growing up, I had no positive examples of what a real man was or how a man was supposed to act and love me until my mother met Jan.

He was the man who stepped into our lives for ten years. He dated my mother, and for the first time, I felt like we were a family. Jan encouraged me to read books and explore science and my creative talents like dancing and singing. In the final years of their relationship, I watched Jan physically hurt my mother when she didn't comply with his demands. Their arguments were loud and disturbing. I always wondered how far things would escalate. I couldn't quite understand how he could be so loving and supportive at times, then turn into a raving, wicked and cruel person. Quite naturally, my distrust in men grew. Yet, through it all, I found a hidden strength – reading therapy, developing a relationship with Jehovah, and leaning on the support of my mom offered me the resilience to survive and reclaim my life.

I dreamed of a life I had only seen in fairytales. Man meets woman; they fall in love, run off into the sunset, build a happy family, buy a house with a white picket fence, and live happily ever after. The world promised security - physically and financially. The romantic TV shows, movies, and love songs I watched and listened to promised happy endings where the good guys win. Yet, when I looked at my reality, I faced physical abuse, poverty, paycheck-to-paycheck living, single motherhood, and running away from one problem after another. In search of love and acceptance, I fell into the arms of men who promised me the world but couldn't deliver.

At 17 years old, I fell for what I thought was a glamorous life, a life out of poverty. There was money, gifts, and all I could ever want. I called him "Woo." He was a slick-talking, fast-life drug dealer. For three years, I thought, *this is the life*. Until I got pregnant. I knew that this would not go over well with Woo. He was already supporting two other women with his kids and expressed that he didn't want any more "mistakes," or he would have them aborted. To avoid the conscious blood guilt of killing an unborn child, I moved away to Atlanta; my mom got a job that transferred her, which was perfect timing for me to move. I had the baby and continued my life. Unfortunately, because I was broken, I continued to attract broken men in my life. I fell into the arms of a real romantic – he was all about me – he wanted me all to himself. At first, I was so relieved to think that someone wanted what I had always wanted. He was a true romantic – wining, dining, and dancing. He made me feel special. For once, I felt loved and wanted, and he wanted me and my son. I eventually moved in with him, and after two years, I got a twofer; I had a husband and a baby girl on the way. It was just like the movies until…

Little did I know, his overly obsessed nature with me was insecurities and jealousy hidden behind his facade. He became more obsessive and controlling. When I didn't respond like he thought I should or let him know my every move, he became outwardly angry, verbally abusive, and eventually physically abusive. He began to isolate me from all those that cared about me. Not allowing me to take phone calls from my family or attend any functions without him.

His violent tendencies only served to re-open the wounds inflicted by my past, leaving me trapped in an all-too-familiar cycle of abuse. One Saturday night, he became so abusive that he struck me in my face; all I could see was red. At that point, I knew I had to leave. On Monday morning, I waited until he went to work, packed up the kids and all our belongings, and drove across the country – not knowing where I was going or what I would do. I called my friend, who, thank God, offered me a job opportunity at a software company, and I ended the journey in Texas.

I was 38, a newly divorced, single mother of two (my son, Corey, and daughter, Summer), living in my mother's one-bedroom apartment, sleeping on her couch. I felt that I had reached an all-time low in my life. I knew it was time for me to do something radically different. My daughter was eight years old at the time, and my son was 16. The kids accepted the arrangement, as they had witnessed the chaos in the marital relationship. They ended up with two peaceful homes to live and thrive in because of the co-parenting relationship.

Through life coaching and associating with people who saw the value in me I had buried for years and a deep desire to heal, I went through a transformative journey of self-discovery and growth. There were two exercises that changed the trajectory of my life. The first was to write a letter to the person I needed to forgive, read it aloud, and then destroy it. What was birthed was a heartfelt and sincere letter to my six-year-old self. I promised her that I would protect her, listen to her voice, and help her live a full life authentically and unapologetically. I've kept that promise. The second exercise was to write a list of my proudest accomplishments and celebrate myself. This exercise reminded me of how skilled and talented I am. I was inspired to pursue other dreams and aspirations that I had set aside due to fear, self-limiting beliefs, or other's opinions. I started acting and entertaining, then writing, which led to award-winning plays and film projects.

I decided to write a book, a book that would tell my story. At that time, I had to reveal the long-lost secret I had held for almost 30 years. My mother had a hard time accepting this and blamed herself for not protecting me. My brother, Corey, was shot and killed during an attempted robbery on Oct 11, 1995. The store owner shot him after a struggle over the gun my brother was using to rob the store. Corey's so-called friend and mastermind of the operation left him to bleed to death on the cold pavement. He was pronounced dead on arrival at the hospital. So, with Corey no longer being alive, she couldn't even confront him and chastise him. It took Mom several months to talk about it again with me. Six months, to be exact. She invited me out to breakfast and said she wanted to talk. She started with an apology, which I warmly accepted and didn't know I needed. The rest of the conversation was a beautiful exchange of encouragement and honesty that led to compassion and understanding.

I did not realize it at the time, but this exchange was the missing piece in my continued healing and reclaiming of my life. Lots of the pain and distrust were entangled in my little eight-year-old thoughts about where my mom was when I needed her most. I needed to hear her side; I needed to forgive her and to forgive myself. My mother, however, had not acknowledged or dealt with her past trauma of abandonment, foster care, drug addiction, etc. Our conversation revealed that it was time to get help to begin her healing process. Mom's journey continues.

For me, after counseling and life coaching, I chose writing and acting as my outlet to heal and overcome the trauma from my past. After being single for four years, I decided to focus on healing from past traumas and created my own set of non-negotiable values, with the love of God as my top priority. I knew that if I did not establish boundaries and ideals to govern myself and the expectations of others, I would allow others to run amuck in my life over and over again. During that time of singleness, I was determined not to marry again.

Then, as if guided by destiny's gentle hand, I crossed paths with Shannon. His presence in my life was unlike anything I had ever known before. With his unwavering patience, compassion, and understanding, he shattered the chains of my past trauma and offered me the chance to rediscover myself. Life can often surprise us when we least expect it. After a concert, my friends and I went to a local lounge. It was there that I met Shannon, a handsome, built bouncer. He flirted, smiled, and asked for my number, which sparked a new possibility. For the first time in four years, I entertained the idea of dating again. I knew the decision to be exclusive wasn't easy. You see, Shannon was running away from a monogamous relationship. He, too, had his share of disappointing relationships; ripe with unfaithfulness, mental illness, and conniving, manipulating women. Together, Shannon and I embarked on a journey of healing, as we nurtured each other's wounds and reignited the flames of hope. With every passing day, my spirit was renewed, and a newfound love blossomed from the ashes of my turbulent past. Two years later, we were married, and we continue to enjoy our marriage. He's an amazing stepfather to our kids and the best husband I could've ever attracted. It was as if Jehovah God pierced my heart and molded him just for me. I had prayed specifically for a man who loved God first; therefore, God would show him how to love me the right way, with lovingkindness, honesty, communication, and faithfulness. I believed wholeheartedly my prayer would be answered. And it was!

Affirmation Thoughts

To all the courageous women who have endured the unimaginable, my story is a testament to the inherent strength that lies within us all. True love is possible, even after experiencing past trauma. It may seem like a far-off dream, but when we least expect it, the universe aligns to bring us the love and healing we deserve.

Today, I am a survivor, not defined by my past but empowered by the strength I have found within myself. Shannon's love and understanding have shown me that the scars we carry do not make us any less worthy of experiencing the overwhelming joy that true love brings.

So, dear warriors, do not lose hope. The journey to healing and restoration may be arduous, but the destination is one worth reaching. Embrace the light within you, and let it guide you to a love that will honor and cherish the beautiful soul that resides within you.

Kimberly Noel Sweet

Kimberly Noel Sweet is an Emmy-nominated, national award-winning journalist, published author, and businesswoman. She completed her undergraduate studies at UCLA and earned a Master of Science degree from the Medill School of Journalism at Northwestern University. Kimberly has worked as an Adjunct Professor at both Jackson State University and Tougaloo College. She was an Anchor, Investigative Reporter, and Managing Editor at WLBT-TV3 over an 11-year span at the station. Her work has been honored by the Associated Press, Mississippi Association of Broadcasters, National Association of Television Producers and Editors, The National Academy of Television Arts and Sciences, as well as community organizations. Kimberly is a multi-media journalist and storyteller who works in print, video, and film.

When Rejection Calls
- Don't Answer!

Kimberly Noel Sweet

Listen to me, you islands; hear this, you distant nations:
Before I was born the LORD called me;
from my mother's womb he has spoken my name.
Isaiah 49:1 (NIV)

It was easily the best night of my eight-year-old life. Until it was the worst.

It was the best because I found myself outside The Forum, Inglewood, California's fabulous event spot. Living down the street from this superstructure, I saw it each day and often dreamed about what happened inside. Round, red, and styled with huge, white columns reaching toward the sky, The Forum held every major sport and entertainment event of its day. From a child's perspective, it looked like a giant merry-go-round. As a birthday present, I was finally going to go inside for a ride. I know my mom was excited, too, because she drove my stepfather's black and gold Cadillac. After what seemed to be an eternity parking the car (and the longest line of people that I had ever seen waiting to get in, we finally went inside. I was wearing a brand-new orange plaid dress and patent leather shoes. My hair had been freshly pressed and pulled into two ponytails held in place by new floral plastic barrettes. I was excited and glad once we finally got to our seats. I couldn't keep still, though; I kept tapping my shoes against the seat in front of me.

When the lights dimmed, a hush fell over the crowd. I tightly held my mom's hand, and when the stage lit up, and the music started, she lifted me to stand on the seat so that I could see above the heads, hands, and bodies blocking my view of The Jackson Five. Jackie, Jermaine, Tito, Marlon, and, yes, Michael, weren't just on my record player or television screen anymore. They were live and in person, a few rows ahead of me, singing their hit, "I Want You Back." Jumping up and down while alternately screaming and singing along, I found my magic moment inside that special place.

Hours later, my best day quickly became my worst. Not long after arriving home, I was dragging a cardboard toy suitcase filled with mismatched clothes and toys into the night after my mother and I were forced out of the house. All my joy and excitement quickly transformed into fear and dread. Listening to the angry cursing, tears, and slamming doors, I hoped that a limousine with The Jackson Five would pull up to rescue us so that we could ride off and stay at their house. As we rode away, I looked out the back window. There was no limo, and The Forum, by then, was empty and dark.

Of all my childhood memories, that night returns to me often. For decades, I linked my birthday with the demise of my mother's marriage to a man who was not my father. Was it really my fault? No one ever said that to me, but they didn't have to. I was born out of wedlock, and my biological father made a point of moving on and never looking back. With me in her arms, my mother didn't have that option.

"You need a husband," my grandma told her, "and she (meaning me) needs a father."

Ever obedient, my mother accepted the proposal of the very next man she dated. The photo of me as a toddler sitting on the front row of their wedding all alone said it all. A baby blue organza bow and dress could not hide the confusion and isolation on my young face.

Our instant family took shape, with each of us playing our assigned part. I still spent a lot of time with Grandma. He went to work. Mom did her best to create a home. As if there wasn't enough to overcome when we moved into a two-bedroom, one-bathroom house in Inglewood, we also integrated the neighborhood. As our boxes were unpacked, an elderly White neighbor was stacking hers at the door. Incredibly polite, she invited us to lunch - chicken salad and grapes - which I didn't eat because an ant was crawling on the edge of the plate.

From the outside, everything seemed fine—even great. My mother's husband had a well-paying job selling furniture in West Los Angeles, so we had new living room and bedroom furniture every year. Usually, a truck dropped off the items, and they were reassembled just as they had been arranged at the store. Sometimes. I would come home, and my entire bedroom would be different. I was literally living on the showroom floor—empty dresser drawers, paper-stuffed pillows, fake books, and strange dolls pushed me out of the space. I eventually realized that our family life had the same showroom prop dynamic.

As the child brought to the marriage, I was often reminded by my mother's new husband that I was an outsider and didn't belong. When I had trouble learning to count, he laughed and told me, "You're stupid and won't ever amount to anything." When a friend of his brought me a puppy from his large litter, I was so excited. Having something of my own to play with, fuss over, and bring me joy gave me an escape I needed from the silence and sadness that hung heavy over our household. It did not last long. After growing close to the puppy for about a month, my stepfather came home early one day and, without ceremony or warning, walked over to the box where the puppy slept, picked it up, and walked out the door. "I really don't want a dog in my house; I'm giving it away," he said on the way out the door. During summer breaks, I was dropped off with his nieces, who were a couple of years older than I was. "You are not our real cousin," the older girl would remind me. The rejection was not just from children. Their grandmother also made a difference between those who were her grandchildren and those who were not. She told my mother, "Make sure she brings her own food. There isn't anything extra here for her."

This was exacerbated when my younger sister was born, and my mother's husband finally had his own child. If there was any doubt that I was treated differently, there certainly was no question after her birth. As an infant, she received the dollhouse and the Black Baby Chrissy doll I wanted for Christmas. I was punished when she lost a pacifier or bottle. More importantly, she never had to bring her own food when we were kept by relatives.

As a young child, I worked hard to become invisible. Didn't say a lot. Didn't ask for much. Didn't remind the new family that I was still around. Shrinking came at a real cost. I was plagued with nightmares (later identified as repressed anxiety). In my dreams, I was always falling—from skyscrapers, out of airplanes, or over cliffs. My screams were never heard, and even when I knew I was dreaming, I struggled to get out of them. I would wake up with my hands tightly gripping the bed rails.

So many subtle words and actions directed toward me screamed that I wasn't worthy. I was told that I wasn't smart, that I didn't deserve things that made me happy, and that I was somehow less than other people in my immediate circle. Yes, I had a loving mother who did all that she could to protect me and make me feel loved and special. But she was working hard to keep a difficult marriage together. I am sure she thought that providing a good home for me was much more important than kind words. Besides that, she was subjected to much worse, so I never complained to her about what was said. I simply accepted it.

After The Jackson Five concert, we moved in with my grandmother in the middle of the night. After regular failed attempts at reconciliation, mostly aimed at maintaining a relationship with my younger sister, we moved out for good when I was 12. We walked away with just our clothes, but the freedom and light were invaluable. My beautiful mother smiled again. Her laughter made everything good, even when we struggled financially. New schools and a fresh environment also helped me to see myself differently.

Mrs. Moreno, my sixth-grade teacher at Arlington Heights Elementary School, encouraged me to read and write poetry. She told me that I should probably become a doctor or a lawyer because I was so smart. Her mother, Mrs. Zack, taught music twice a week and encouraged me to learn to play the cello and sing in the choir. She told me I was a very gifted young person. Having a person in authority believe in me, encourage me, and lavish praise and attention on me was an experience I had never had before. There was no ridicule, only praise and support. I began to invest in myself, learning to play the cello and write poetry. I worked hard to become the person I was learning to believe I could be.

Rather than athletics or other extracurricular activities, which would put too much of a strain on my mom, I spent time at the public library. The local librarian helped me choose great books to read and ultimately gave me a special certificate because I read every book in the young adult reading section. She told me my love for reading would really help me in college, something I never knew about or considered before then. When the local public school became unsafe, my grandmother helped pay tuition for a nearby small Catholic school. Their school-mandated standardized tests proved my hard work was worth it. I was one of three non-Catholics out of 125 accepted into a private college preparatory school.

My mother also found her own footing, turning a part-time job into a career at the Los Angeles Community College District. Her ability to overcome bad relationships and achieve independence and happiness set an important standard for me. Our closeness as survivors of shared trauma forged a lasting, loving bond.

Amos Christian Methodist Episcopal, the church I chose to join as a teenager because it was a block away from our apartment, gave me a new family that welcomed and supported me in a way that I had never experienced before. I faithfully attended Sunday services and weekday Bible study, where I learned to study the Bible and pray to God. School counselors told me that I should apply to several schools; however, I didn't have the money for multiple applications. I only applied to UCLA, a top national university, because it was close and affordable. I was blessed with acceptance to and attendance at an institution that gave me a glimpse of what was possible. With my church family behind me, rooting and praying for my success, I bravely stepped into my next chapter. Though UCLA was just 30 miles or so from our apartment, for me, it was another world. Nestled between the uber wealthy communities of Beverly Hills and Bel-Air, the campus offered both a window to view and door to enter through to major opportunities which would shape my life.

I interned at CNN in Los Angeles and KCBS-TV. As an editorial writer at the college paper, I won a statewide award at a journalism conference in Hawaii. My poetry was selected for publication in *Westwind, The Campus Journal for the Arts*. At graduation, I was honored to be selected as a Chancellor's Marshall for service to the university community. Ultimately, I would leave sunny Los Angeles for Chicago, The Windy City, to earn a Master of Science Degree from the Medill School of Journalism.

Professionally, that led to work as a television anchor, investigative reporter, published author, documentary producer, college journalism instructor, and business owner. My life has been richly blessed with personal and professional accomplishments, and even more is ahead for me.

As for my biological father - and the man in whose house I lived—both judged me unworthy and sentenced me to a broken existence. But by whose authority? Surely not God's! What a blessing to finally discover as an adult that God Himself chose me, kept me surrounded by a hedge of protection, and stored up blessings beyond measure for me. I was never physically harmed or abused. By all objective medical standards and implied social norms, I grew up healthy both physically and emotionally. The quiet house spurred a love for reading, which increased my intellect, knowledge, and critical thinking skills. Keeping to myself also spared my exposure to gangs, crime, and teen pregnancy, which plagued so many around me. I was not cursed; I was blessed and set apart! Life has taught me to tune out others and instead believe what God says about me and who He says I am. After many years, I have rejected rejection and embraced my value as God's unique creation.

When I see people at the occasional wedding or funeral who knew me as a child—and rejected me—to them, I am rightly unrecognizable. It was in fact true that they had never seen me at all. But God had seen me and called me by name my whole life. From this point, I see that what some meant for evil, God used to bless me. He allowed me to experience hurt and rejection at an early age so that I could fully embrace the only real acceptance that matters—my true identity as a child of God, perfectly made by Him to brightly shine in this life until I join Him and my foremothers in heaven.

God's blessings keep coming. The child who was evicted out of one house by a stepfather on her eighth birthday, now owns several properties. I have been married for more than 30 years with a family of my own. As a journalist, I've won national honors for stories that spoke for children caught in drugs and prostitution around their elementary school. None of this is an accident, but rather God's continually unfolding divine plan. When my nightmares ended, my dreams began. In finding my voice, God gave me a platform as a journalist to speak for others who cannot speak for themselves or who need to know that their lives and concerns matter. I see myself so often in the faces and lives of others. With support, I believe that any person can blossom into what they were meant to be. As a young woman, I was also blessed to have my grandmother, Mary B. Smith, either walk me to school, wait for me at the bus stop, or meet me at

Winchell's Donuts every day until her health dictated otherwise. She taught me to cut up a whole chicken, balance a checkbook, and organize her medication. During these life lessons, I also gleaned her wisdom about life, love, and becoming whole.

God used teachers, a librarian, and my own female relatives to build my confidence and speak a different message to me about who I was. No longer the child seeking invisibility, I began to dream out loud about what my life could be, and I started working toward making those dreams come true.

I know the power of support. Without it, those who I see myself in might not be able to blossom. But the world needs all of our gifts and voices. Perhaps more importantly, as a stepmother myself, I have worked tirelessly to be the exact opposite of what I experienced. I tell my "bonus son" how proud I am of him. I made sure that he was equally provided for and included whenever he was able to spend time with us. Whether he was disciplined for throwing a wild party while I was out of town or praised for achieving honors, he has always known that he is loved and that he is my family.

When I consider my long-term service to middle school girls and my relationship with my family, I am grateful for the difficult experiences I've had. I'm not sure who I would be without them. I also know that when I packed that little cardboard suitcase, what was really inside was all that I would need to sustain me and put me onto my life's path.

Losing my grandmother in college and my mother in July 2021 left significant voids in my life, but I still hear them asking what's going on with my properties and why my documentary isn't finished yet. Their voices are part of the chorus calling my name - smart, successful, and loved. I will hear them and feel them with me until I meet them again.

Reflection:

When you face hardships, can you see God's divine hand leading you through the tough times to a better, more blessed place?

Do you believe what people say about you, even those close to you or in authority over you, or what God says? How do your actions reflect what you say you believe?

Affirmative Prayer:

Father God, I thank You for this journey we walk together and the purpose You have planted within me. I know that each and every part of it has been carefully ordained by You. What a blessing that Jesus has already endured and overcome every hardship and rejection that I could ever encounter and that the Holy Spirit stands ready to act upon the power of God's Word to bring me every victory in this life! May every young woman who feels rejected find true love and acceptance in You. Amen.

Psalm 118:22-23 (NIV)

The stone the builders rejected has become the cornerstone. The Lord has done this, and it is marvelous in our eyes.

Just Write

Tonee B. Shelton

Tonee B. Shelton is a poet and author who enjoys creating poetry for live readings to engage people and inspire others to believe in themselves. She has written three volumes of poetry, *In Search of Freedom* (2021), *Identity Crisis* (2022), and *Remnants* (2023), and is finishing up her first book of prose, *No One is Coming to Save You*, a call to action for everyone to embrace their gifts and unique talents to create the life they desire. She has her own Instagram series, "Let Me Tell You Something," where she gives brief tips and tricks on how to keep a positive mindset when pursuing dreams. She also designs shirts, stickers, and coffee mugs underneath her brand, Bettawatchyatone. Keep up with Tonee on social media!

Instagram: toneebshelton
Facebook: Toneebshelton
website: www.bettawatchyatone.com

Oops Upside Ya Head!

Tonee B. Shelton

David said to Saul, "Let no one lose heart on account of this
Philistine; your servant will go and fight him."
1 Samuel 17:32 (NIV)

I watched the blood drip down the side of his ugly face. Every
person knows their breaking point, and at the ripe age of ten, I
realized that being kind to people intent on harming you is not
effective. Some call handing out what you are getting matching
energy; I call it letting people know that I am nothing to be
messed with.

My parents did not condone violence. In fact, they always
encouraged me to "use my words;" to stop, think, look, and listen before I spoke. My mother was so focused on molding me
into a good human that she put a WWJD (what would Jesus do)
band around my wrist.

Each morning, as she kissed my cheek, the lip liner on her
lips bleeding onto the side of my face, she would ask, "Tonee, we
are going to have a good day, right?"

To which I would promptly respond, "Yes, ma'am."

She would ask, "And when we feel ourselves getting hyper, we are going to look at our band and ask ourselves...?"

"What would Jesus do!" I would loudly proclaim.

Yet, before she crossed the threshold of the door to lead me outside, I was into things. What can I say? I was a high-energy kid, or what my pops would say, "full of fluid and ready to do it."

As a child, I loved playing, reading, and running. The highlight of my day was lunchtime because we got to eat and then play outside. My world revolved around running, jumping, and playing.

There was one part of my youth that made school days particularly difficult. As much as I loved school and learning, the kids at school did not have the same love for me. I found myself the butt of every joke. My clothes and hairstyles were picked apart, and I rarely had someone to push me on the swing. Any activity that required two or more people was foreign to me. My class took every opportunity to treat me badly.

Like all great bullying organizations, the ringleader of the bunch – Joshua - went out of his way to make my life a living hell every day, multiple times a day. I could not have escaped him, even if I tried! I tried to avoid him like the plague, but when I would relax and start playing freely, I would hear an annoying voice in the distance chant, "Bowhead, bowhead, she ain't got no forehead!" The insides of my stomach would clench up, and I would prepare myself for fifteen minutes of torture.

I am sure my teachers knew about the bullying because I often complained to my parents about not having friends and that one person made everyone else hate me. This behavior was happening during a time when adults allowed students to hash out their own problems. There were no anti-bullying campaigns or safe spaces for students in the 90s.

I always wondered what it was about me that brought out the worst in others. I tried to be nice to everyone I met. My parents raised me to say "yes ma'am and no sir" to my elders, yet when I did that, I could hear snickers from my peers. It seemed as though all the things that my parents instilled in me; the bullies made fun of. I was not mature enough to understand the concept of jealousy and envy. I would have never understood at the age of 10 that perhaps the main bully in my life had a crush on me yet was not emotionally mature enough to express interest in a healthy way. All I knew was that I was fed up with being made fun of and feeling low, and someone was going to pay.

The final straw came when we were out on a field trip to the zoo, and Joshua began taunting me again, "Look at Tonee. She's a roach. She belongs at this zoo as an exhibit."

I froze. Everyone around me was doubling over in laughter. I fought hard to hold back the tears behind my glasses. I had no idea where my teacher was. All I knew was that I was done being everyone's proverbial whipping girl. I had promised myself that the next time Josh said or did anything to me, I was going to physically respond.

I had been expressing my frustration about Joshua to my parents, and they had complained to my teacher and the principal about intentionally degrading and aggressive behavior towards me. Nothing was ever done about it. My father had the bright idea of giving me one of his green army notebooks. He suggested that I write down each time Joshua irritated me, so that there was a record of his bullying. Although I thought the idea was a bit silly, I respected my father and was desperate for some type of intervention for my grief.

One day, we were getting ready to line up for lunch, and I was headed toward my usual spot at the back of the line when I heard the phrase, "Roach, roach, Tonee is a roach." Then I heard the snickers that were so familiar to me. I momentarily paused to remind myself what my mother said in the morning. "What would Jesus do?" I then thought about my father's very mature but unrealistic suggestion to journal my thoughts in his green book. Joshua's voice cut into my thoughts like a razor. I had grown weary of him calling me an insect.

"Roach! Roach! Tonee is a roach!" He yelled again. Before I knew it, I placed both hands on my father's green leather-bound book; I raised that book above my head as far as my 10-year-old arms would stretch, and I brought that book down on Joshua's skull with the force of one thousand men.

You could hear a rat lick ice in that classroom after the book connected. All I remember is him screaming in pain, blood sliding down the side of his face from the book breaking his skin, and the widened looks of horror from the rest of my class.

I was immediately sent to the principal's office. Because there was so much documentation of my complaints about Joshua, the principal made the decision not to formally write me up. He recommended instead that I go home for the rest of the day. That was the best nap of my life. And while my parents weren't exactly thrilled about me fighting boys or fighting at all, my father did tell me later on that night that he was proud of me for standing up for myself. He said something else that will forever resonate with me.

"Now that you've shown you are not afraid, ain't nobody going to mess with you."

I went to bed sure that not only would the other kids mess with me but that it was going to be ten times worse since I had physically assaulted their leader. Either way, my sleep was great, and I was not the least bit remorseful. A funny thing happened the following day in class. No one bothered me the entire day. When we ate lunch, there were no jokes about my clothes or my hairstyle. I even got to play four-square without being heckled. Of course, Joshua was absent. I overheard the teacher at lunch mention that he had a concussion and would be out for two days. I would at least get 48 hours of peace.

When I got home from school, my dad asked me how things went, to which I gleefully responded that I had a wonderful day and added that Joshua was absent. He laughed and said once more, "I have a feeling that Joshua is not going to be a problem."

The following day was even more peaceful than the first. One of my classmates even asked me to play two-square. I learned the power of influence then and that people are followers. I appreciated the attention, but I knew that it was predicated on Joshua's absence and that when he returned, things would go back to being horrendous.

That night, I tossed and turned. My father and I had done our customary prayers, but I could not nod off to dreamland. How could I when I knew that the sole instigating source for my torture would be in class the next day? I imagined everyone picking up where they left off before his absence, making me the butt of every joke and ignoring my existence. I couldn't sleep because I knew that school the next day was going to be terrible.

As my mother kissed my cheek the next morning and sealed the deal with her customary "What would Jesus do?" question, I quickly nodded in agreement. I hoped Jesus would intercede on my behalf and keep Joshua at bay. As I walked slowly to my class, my heart hammered through my ears. I imagined this was how David must have felt as he approached Goliath, really nervous but determined to finish what he had started. As I walked through the door and locked eyes with Joshua, I held my breath for a second. I was prepared to thrash him again if he pushed me to it. He stared at me and then turned his gaze back to the front of the class. He didn't interact with me at lunch or during recess. There were no snarky comments about my outfit. It was as if I did not exist. Not only that, but Joshua did not say much of anything to anyone. I was floored. Maybe the new Joshua was a clone! Either way, I remembered what my pops said and knew he was right. I had conquered my Goliath. Joshua had fallen.

When my pops picked me up from school, he smiled after he kissed me. He then inquired, "How was Joshua today?"

"Quiet," I responded. "Not only did he not bother me, but he didn't say anything much to anyone. He didn't even raise his hand to answer questions."

My dad laughed. "Little girl, your days of being bullied are over."

He was right. In fact, Joshua didn't speak to me for the remainder of the year. I even made friends. It was awesome.

Why did I share this childhood story? Because it was a pivotal moment in my life where I had to rely on God to face my demons head-on. I am not telling you to punch, hit, smack, or cut someone, (because you will go to jail), but I am telling you that avoiding problems does not free you from them. I was being bullied and had tried everything from asking for help from parents and teachers to trying to draw less attention to myself. Nothing changed until I went right upside Joshua's head, much like David attacked the Philistine.

"Reaching into his bag and taking out a stone, he slung it and struck the Philistine in the forehead. The stone sank unto his forehead, and he fell face down on the ground." 1 Samuel 17: 49 (NIV)

David was a mere boy when he struck down Goliath. He was young, small in stature, and maybe even afraid. But what David showed us is that faith in God and the courage to address the giants (or, in my case, the bully) in your life will ultimately set you free.

God has a purpose for each one of us, but it cannot be revealed until we rely on Him and leverage His strength to address and attack any situation that threatens to diminish our existence or minimize our power. Being a victim of bullying was hard for me. It brought me a ton of pain and anguish, and even now, as an adult, I sometimes still feel like that 10-year-old girl who didn't have friends and was afraid to stand up for herself. Now that I am older and wiser, I remind myself to tap into the energy that I channeled to go upside Joshua's head, and I am suddenly able to execute whatever vision I have and to properly address whoever (and whatever) stands in the way of accomplishing my goals.

God brought me through bullying as a child, and I am confident that He will continue to bring me through any and every obstacle as long as I continue to have faith in Him. God brought me through insecurity in high school, depression in college, and financial instability after graduate school. At varying points in my life, giants stood between me and God's purpose. It was in those moments that I had to tap into my faith in Him. Faith in God alleviates fear. Maybe you are in a season of indecision, fear, or even avoidance. I know that when I am in these seasons, I reflect on my Joshua experience, and I exhaust all options before I bust my problems upside the head. Ultimately, you will not win favor with God being violent, but your faith is the strength needed to overcome everything. In college, when I realized that I was depressed, I prayed and asked God for help. Help came in the form of my speaking with a therapist, joining a girls' group on campus, and having honest conversations about where I was mentally and emotionally. It was moving in vulnerability (which for me was terrifying), yet another giant that I had to face if I wanted to be well.

You can and will overcome your demons, and when you face them head-on, they become small. Joshua became small to me after our incident. Prior to me facing him, he became like a god (or an oversized Philistine), and I felt like a small teenager. Feeling small made me act small. When I thought big, I acted big, and then it revealed just how small and insignificant Joshua and his antics really were. God is bigger than any temporary setback that we can ever face. And like my earthly father and mother, who encouraged and loved me but did not intercede on my behalf while I was being bullied, I am thankful that they revealed to me the importance of grit, tenacity, and being bold by allowing me to grow through that experience. God will use you when you operate in boldness. Tell that bully in your life, "Boy bye," and if they still don't move, well, you know my philosophy. Be bold. Let God use you.

Operating in God's purpose for me means that I'm bigger than all my enemies. I was too young to understand the concept that whatever we focus on grows. When we are children, the classroom can seem like our entire world. Before I fought my bully, I focused all of my time and energy on him. I hid from him, thought about him when I was away from school, and talked about him when I was home. I allowed him to take up all of this free mental space in my young brain when, instead, I should have focused on addressing him the first time he treated me badly and then moved on. I allowed other kids' thoughts about him to guide and manipulate my behavior instead of focusing on the one or two people who genuinely liked me for me, not for what other people thought. When we ignore things, they sprout legs and run amuck! We have a purpose in life, but we can't get to that purpose without some Philistines or bullies that stand in our path. Now that I am in my thirties, and Josh is a thing of the past, I often see moments where something stands in my way, induces fear within me, and I succumb to the temptation to avoid it. It is in these moments that I have to revive that brave elementary school girl who went upside her problem's head. The difference is that I no longer wait around to see if my bully will leave on its own.

I implore you to take the time right now to reflect on the giants and bullies in your life. What is that thing that is standing in the way of God's purpose for you? Who is that person that you avoid like the plague? Who is cumbersome and downright nasty to you? What is that project that you've been avoiding or the tough conversation you have been putting off for years? It is all of the things that I just mentioned that are the Goliaths, or Joshuas in your life that stand in the way of you getting everything that God desires for you. Facing our fears head on is scary in the moment, but a requirement to get to the peace that we desire. Get free today. I believe in you.

Facing your demons head on sets a trend for others to do the same. Just as I mentioned, the students in my class treated me differently after I hit Joshua. People will treat you differently once they see that you live a bold, purposeful life. As much as we love to think that we are these dynamic human beings who think for ourselves and do things without the opinions of others, we are often sheep looking for shepherds to think, direct and guide us. David could have been like his people, fearful of something because of what the group thought. However, he believed in his abilities, relied on his faith in God and went against the group's doubts and teasing to save his people. When you face your fears directly, those around you will gain more respect for you, and eventually imitate your behavior. Ever notice the domino effect of influence in friendship groups? One person writes a book, or becomes a public speaker, or starts their own business, and then slowly, others in the group do the exact same thing or similar things. Ever notice how people get into new relationships and then suddenly start going to church, or dressing or speaking differently, or doing things that they have never done before? *We act like the people that we are around!* Many of us are simply waiting for one person to be brave, to be a shepherd, and demonstrate what life can be like when we live freely. You are the David in your family, community, workspace, sorority, town, and church. No pressure or anything, but you are the key to unlocking a generation of other people by your behavior. Imitation is the greatest form of flattery.

Reflection:

What giants are currently in your life that need to be faced?

What makes you feel powerful?

An Affirmative Prayer:

The giants in my life may appear big,
but my God is bigger
He created me to live a life filled with purpose,
and all that comes with bold living, means addressing
giants, whose shoes are merely a figment of my imagination
once I try them on for size.

Lord, I know that You created me for big things. You knew me before I even knew myself. Please keep me focused, not on what humans say about me, but on what You are requiring of me. Allow my fear to become a footrest. Allow my faith to chart a path towards favor. Allow me to address the things in my life that keep me afraid, for when I address my fears, I set myself free to grow. In Jesus' name, amen.

Just Write

Velena L. McRae

Velena L. McRae is an award-winning leader, visionary, speaker, and philanthropist with three decades of experience in the governmental sector. She currently works for the Treasury Department, where she is a member of the Leadership Cadre in the Communications Stakeholder Liaison Field Division, which focuses on the local engagement of the payroll and tax practitioner community to ensure tax compliance. Velena is also a member of the Communications Media Cadre and gives interviews to news outlets as warranted.

Velena is the Founder and President of the JV McRae Foundation, which actively serves the community by providing resources to support education, health, financial, and family stability initiatives. Velena is passionate about selflessly giving of her time, talent, and treasures to empower and uplift the lives of others. She serves on the Board of the Ivy & Pearl Foundation of Dallas, a Past President of Alpha Kappa Alpha Sorority, Incorporated, Alpha Xi Omega Chapter, and a Friend of the African American Museum-Dallas.

Velena received her Master of Business Administration from the University of Arkansas – Little Rock and Business Analytics Certification from Texas A& M – Commerce. She also holds a Bachelor of Science in Accounting from the University of Arkansas – Pine Bluff.

Velena was married to Jesse C. McRae III for 29 years before his unexpected passing in February 2020, and she has two adult sons.

This Wasn't My Plan

Velena L. McRae

*"For my thoughts are not your thoughts, neither are your ways
my ways,' declares the LORD. 'As the heavens are
higher than the earth, so are my ways higher than your
ways and my thoughts than your thoughts."*
Isaiah 55:8-9 (NIV)

When I walked into the room, the scent of disinfectant hit my
nose; the room was cold and sterile, and the sound of monitors
beeping was constant. The closer I got, the more I shook in fear.
My heart was beating so fast, and with such strength, I was certain
others could hear it. I had to take a closer look. In my mind, as
long as that beep-beep-beep continued, we would be okay.

As he lay on the table hooked up to various blinking and
beeping machines, I closed my eyes against the harsh operating
room lights and said a silent prayer, "God, please don't take him
from me, not now." I wanted him to open his eyes or, at the
minimum, breathe without the assistance of the ventilator.

We had a running joke. I would always tell him that 'he almost missed me.' And then he would say, in the sexiest way, "No, YOU almost missed me." We met in November 1988, my senior year in college. I couldn't wait to graduate and start my career; getting a boyfriend was the furthest thing from my mind. But he was, as some would say, tall, dark, and handsome. He stood six feet two, with a striking profile, and when he smiled, it would melt your heart. Almost everyone at my small-town HBCU knew of him and made sure to tell me that he was a *good guy*. On the other hand, this was the first time I had heard of him in the three years I had been there.

Trying not to be distracted, but with my interest piqued, I wanted to know more about him. At first glance, he appeared to be a bit nerdy, clean, preppy dressed, and very well-mannered; you know, a "Carlton" [Carlton Banks, the character from the '90s sitcom "Fresh Prince of Bel-Air"]. But as I got to know him, I realized he was 100% "Will" (Will Smith, "Fresh Prince of Bel-Air" character), through and through. Carlton is an upper-class, intelligent, smartly dressed, handsome man whom any parent would be proud to have their daughter marry. Will, on the other hand, is the street-smart cousin who has the swag that makes girls go wild. Will could talk his way out of or into anything. And so could the person I fell in love with. The grown-ups outside his inner circle got the Carlton version, while everyone else got the Will version. We quickly became inseparable, and in a blink, we were in love, a year later married, with a bundle of joy added to our family, and we moved five hours away from all that we knew and loved.

We were young, idealistic, and had no clue; that made it all fun. By this time, our son was hitting the tiresome threes. Those were some learning years for us all. There was nothing we couldn't accomplish together. We were ready to take on the world and make our mark. I had his back, and he had mine. Whatever one person lacked, the other could stand in the gap. About three years later, we welcomed our second son. From that point, we called the boys #1 son and #2 son or, in a hurry, "1-son and 2-son." As our family was growing and experiencing new things, we realized parenting was a task we couldn't adequately prepare for. As the saying goes, life is like a box of chocolates because you don't know what you are going to get.

Like any other relationship, there were difficult times, but we always figured things out. Our catchphrase, repeated often during difficult decisions, was, "God takes care of babies and fools." We were well past the baby age, so we knew which category we fell into.

We were at the season of our lives that some call the empty nest years; however, one of my little birds had finished college and circled back home after graduation. Honestly, we were happy he was back, but we told him he had one year to find himself, and then he had to move out or pay rent. He had the entire second floor of the house to himself and worked late evenings, so we didn't see him much. Just knowing he was home and safe was comforting. When Jesse traveled for work, 2-Son and I would have momma/son time. We vibed and would watch our favorite shows and have our favorite treats.

Just when I thought all was well and life was good, that's when it happened. It was a typical Wednesday; we'd wake up, get ready, and head to work, and after work, he'd run errands or do household/yard chores while I attended a sorority committee meeting. There was no sign of the impending doom that would crash into our lives like a tsunami swallowing everything in its path.

I thought he was asleep when I first saw him but quickly realized something was wrong. I kept calling his name, "Jesse, Jesse!" I thought, *what could this be?* One might typically think heart attack, but this man was at the top of his fitness game. Without pause, I screamed for my son, who was upstairs in his room. I reached for my phone and called 911. Ironically, the ambulance that we pass on a daily basis because the fire station is on the corner was at our home in less than five minutes. The first responders systematically began checking his airway, breathing, and trying to find a pulse. One shouted to the other, "Begin CPR and get the ventilator." I was slightly relieved when they got a pulse. They secured the portable ventilator and prepared to transport him. I threw on some sweatpants and yelled for my son, "2-Son!" who had actually been standing in the doorway of my room the whole time. I grabbed my keys and followed the EMTs. After arriving at the nearest hospital, I jumped out of the car [I think it was probably still running] and ran inside, only to be stopped by staff because they took him into a room where we were not allowed. I sat in the hallway right outside the door while hospital personnel ran in and out of the room - some with machines, some with meds, and some with nothing but intense and concerned looks on their faces. This went on for what seemed an eternity. The doctors finally came out and told me that he was stable, but he was in a medically induced coma [to give the meds and treatment time to work without his resistance.]

Son-1 was called that night. He dropped everything and came home immediately to be by his dad's side. I was happy to see him but wished it was for a more pleasant occasion. For the next six days, there was a stream of friends and family at the hospital and at our home. They brought food, waited, and prayed with and for us.

I opened my eyes, and he looked the same. His eyes were still closed, and the machines were still blinking and beeping. From where I was sitting, I could see the display on the heart monitor even though the doctors had angled the machine away from me. The numbers were dropping, and I knew we only had a sliver of time for God to step in. I held my breath, waiting for my miracle and waiting for my prayer to be answered.

I knew without a doubt that he would wake up, and we would leave the hospital together, and continue our lives. God was listening, right? All my life, I was taught that God is always there; He answers prayers, heals the sick, and raises the dead. As the numbers on the machine continued to drop, I watched and waited for God. But He didn't show up. I didn't get my miracle. My prayer wasn't answered. He didn't open his eyes or breathe without the ventilator. My heart felt like a ton of bricks hit it. My mouth opened, but no words came out; I couldn't believe this was how our story would end. My emotions were all over the place. I was angry, in disbelief, and shocked. That day, I left the hospital without him, and my life was forever changed.

How do you reconcile the instant turn-off of almost 30 years of having someone in your life? I had been with Jesse for over half my life and didn't have a doubt in my mind that we would be together forever. Like our marriage vows said, "till death do us part," but I thought the angel of death would come for us when we were in our nineties, not our fifties. Things were good; both sons had college degrees and were working. We felt confident we had given them the foundation they needed to succeed in life, and we had just hit our prime and were ready to rediscover each other in the next phase of life. But then this.

The first weeks after someone dies, you are so busy with the business of death that you are operating on autopilot. Honestly, I was on autopilot for over a year. During the day, I was constantly moving, going, and doing. At night, I didn't sleep because I was too angry. I was furious at him for dying, indignant at God for not answering my prayers, and to top it off, it was unjust that we didn't get a warning. The Bible says, "in the twinkling of an eye," and it was literally just that. I was mad at the world for continuing to turn or trying to turn.

The entire world came to a complete stop two weeks after the funeral. We were on lockdown because of the COVID-19 pandemic. Not only was I learning to navigate living during a pandemic, but I was also learning to live without my best friend. As horrible as it may sound, I was a little thankful for the pandemic. It allowed me to be alone and come to terms with my new normal. I didn't want the after-a-death rituals or routines like daily visitors, phone calls, or invitations to dinner.

I didn't realize I needed it, but for at least the first year, people would call or text me every single day. Year two and three, I continued to receive periodic but consistent text messages, notes, and cards. I just wanted to be left alone to wallow in my misery. I was beyond depressed; I rarely ate, didn't comb my hair, nor would I leave the house unless warranted. My boys, well, we were all in a state of shock for such a long time that we skipped conversations on how to process. We didn't know what to say to each other. We tiptoed around the subject for months.

At one point, I was okay with closing my eyes and never waking up again… ever. I wouldn't take my life, but if I were to wake up dead one day, I would be okay with it. But God was not fine with it. He gave me assignments that forced me to look past my own situation. I call it the *relict confines*. I was merely surviving in a world where I felt all alone, or at least the only one with these feelings, which were useless in making things better. I gravitated to others who suddenly found themselves members of the same widows' club and quickly realized I wasn't alone; they didn't ask to join this club either.

I made phone calls and sent notes, texts, flowers, and other items of remembrance to people I knew had lost a loved one. For the holidays, I sent special remembrance Thanksgiving and Christmas cards. In the spring, I sent wildflower seed cards shaped like hearts. The receiving person could plant the seed card to remember their loved ones and watch the flowers grow. Utilizing self-help booklets on grief, I shared with others and added a personalized note about my experience. What was the purpose of this? It allowed a glimpse of hope and healing to shine through. Besides, it gave me something to do, kept my mind busy, and let others know they were not alone. One of my sisters and a close friend suggested I seek grief counseling. I was a little leery at first because of the stigma of counseling, but grief therapy was the best decision I could have made.

My aha moment hit when I acknowledged that other grievers had someone who understood what they were going through and, despite the depths of despair, they too would make it, and someone was rooting for them. I walked in this love; it just felt right. I would demonstrate and explain to them all they had to do was live one moment and take one step, one day at a time. In return, we all could assist others through their grief the same way we had been helped, which would also bring healing. In the simplest way, I would allow a small piece of the world inside my confines.

"...who comforts us in all our troubles, so that we can comfort those in any trouble with the comfort we ourselves receive from God."
2 Corinthians 1:4 (NIV)

Am I still grieving? Absolutely. Am I still angry? *Yes*. However, I can't allow myself to wallow in self-pity or be angry 24/7. To work through what can be debilitating emotions, I journal, I read, I focus on what is good, and I keep busy. Do I still want to lie down at night and never wake up again? No. However, I do acknowledge my feelings, and sometimes I cry. But now, instead of crying all night, I only allow myself a moment and follow it with prayer and a happy reminisce of him. The reality is there are still many things to be done in this life. I want to go places I have never been, travel the world, see God's wondrous works, and do what I have committed to my vision board. The drawback plaguing me is that I have to do it without him, and that definitely was not my plan.

It took me a minute; I had to weigh my odds as to whether I wanted to remain in an unhappy emotional state enveloped in self-pity or live life, one day at a time, grateful. With or without me, life still goes on. It's like a high-stakes card game; I must play the cards I was dealt. Somedays, I feel it is the worst hand ever -- seeing couples living my dream, eating my cake, and taking my trips, and it hurts down to the core. We often develop a lens of the world centered and shaped by our previous experiences and beliefs. Any straying from that view of ourselves and others taints our ability to be free in the now. Then, there are other days when I feel like I've been dealt a pretty good hand living in the moment, sharing the memories with family and friends, making decisions based on desires, relinquishing fear, and doing things because I want to, and for that, I **am** grateful.

My world has been turned upside down. All that I ever hoped for is no longer. The hopes and dreams for our future together died that day in a cold, sterile operating room amid blinking and bleeping machines. What do I do now? Where do

I go from here? Life doesn't always go as planned. It is easy to fall into a depth of despair and withdraw into a cocoon where we don't have to experience life anymore. But that is not God's plan. During my decline, I felt the presence of God saying to me, "You almost missed me." Quite the irony, pushing the world aside and protecting my space, I almost forgot the one thing that has continued to be there for me through it all. All I know to do is to keep walking by faith and know beyond a shadow of a doubt that God's got my back. Regardless of what happens in life, you have to keep going and trusting that God's plan is the best plan. *"For we walk by faith, not by sight." 2 Corinthians 5:7 (NKJV)*

Reflection:

How can you live your life more intentionally and abundantly each day, knowing that tomorrow is not promised?

An Affirmative Prayer:

"When you pass through the waters, I *will* be with you; And through the rivers, they shall not overflow you. When you walk through the fire, you shall not be burned, Nor shall the flame scorch you. For I *am* the LORD your God, The Holy One of Israel, your Savior..." Isaiah 43;2-3 (NKJV)

Velena L. McRae

Just Write

163

Dr. Michelle Kindred

Dr. Michelle Kindred's inner beauty is centered on giving and being a lover of Christ. Academically/professionally, she is an author, freelance writer, substantive copy/contributing editor, and educator. As a Professor of Education Leadership, Science Teaching Methods - Master and Ph.D.-level scholars, she teaches, mentors, and supports new teachers and principals through field supervision and guidance in unveiling their true potential and making a meaningful contribution to the field of education.

Dr. Kindred is the sole proprietor of Intentional Matters, LLC, where she extends her mentorship through her services as an Intentional Matters' Life Coach. Her philosophy is driven by practicing intentionality, mindfulness, existential well-being, and recognizing our God-given purpose.

She is the executive leader and owner of Cooper Kindred Ventures, LLC, which supports the underrepresented and black communities through mentoring, educational resources, professional development, and well-being. Additionally, Dr. Kindred and CKV, LLC offer support through her Non-profit foundation, *The Red Cardinal Experience (TRCE)*. The RCE-nonprofit foundation supports God-inspired visions and dreams of Black entrepreneurs/visionaries and businesses through fundraising, philanthropic efforts, donations, and sponsorships.

The RCE also procures the Mary L. Cooper Memorial Scholarship [in honor of her mother – a former educator and counselor], which provides scholarship opportunities to graduating high school seniors majoring in education, counseling, and humanities *and* adults transitioning from alternate careers to education teaching and counseling.

Dr. Michelle Kindred is an active member of Alpha Kappa Alpha Sorority, Inc.®, continuing her mentorship and service throughout the Dallas community. She is married to her knight, Bryan K. Kindred, of 31 years and blessed with two exceptional children.

To learn more about Dr. Kindred and her inspiration for My Story, Your Hope, visit the TRCE website, Facebook, and Instagram for a recorded interview and insight into the author and co-author's journey as they tell their stories.

Rediscovering Me

Michelle Kindred

"Believe in yourself and all that you are. Know that there is something inside you that is greater than any obstacle."
Christian D. Larson, American teacher

Overwhelmed by the herds of people talking, eating, and reminiscing. I retreated to my room. I could still hear the clamor and decided to move to a quieter space – the solitude of my closet. Lying on the closet floor, curled up in a fetal position, I cried uncontrollably. Blubbering sobs of indistinguishable words, "Where are you, where are you, why did you leave me? I can't do this; I don't want to be here anymore." I sat up and began trying to console myself with a wildly rhythmic rock, back and forth, back and forth.

Suddenly, I felt a warm sensation and pressure around me, as if something or someone had embraced me and tried to pause my rocking. Time seemed to stand still. I felt like I had an out-of-body experience. Could it be? The only perceivable answer was a touch from my mom. I wanted to think that God allowed her to visit me once more before her final ascent to be with Him. She would finally be at peace and in a place without fear, no harm, stress, or worry.

I will never forget that morning; my eyes were barely opened but I was startled by movement in the room. It was just before the sun had peaked over the horizon, a chill was in the air, and my mom and sisters were rushing around, pulling clothes out of drawers, stripping dresses off hangers, and throwing everything from shoes, coats, and toothbrushes into garbage bags. I was confused, but my sister said, "Get all the stuff you want to take with you; we are going away and might not come back." My dad had left for work; he usually left before sunrise and came home late at night.

"Is daddy coming?" I whispered. With a silent and slow head shake from side to side, my sister, staring me dead in the eye, motioned no. We packed the car and drove away.

Picture a child witnessing a broken family, a struggling single parent, and siblings who responded negatively to the pain and confusion of divorce—the typical experiences of family instability and exposure to innocuous change. Being the youngest of four girls, I witnessed firsthand three variations of adolescent egocentrism and the actions and reactions to it from each parent. It seemed like their behavior got worse after we moved. For my siblings, this included breaking the rules, avoiding the truth, or, as some would say, "little white lies," selfishness, manipulation, and plain old being a kid. We were never straight-out disrespectful to our parents, but the disrespect showed up in other ways. Small and insignificant, simple teenage disobedience and trespasses.

However, the effects were compounded when three young girls systematically perpetuated disobedience; specifically, one night, I heard my sister get up from her bed. I watched her remove her nightgown, and to my dismay, she had on a hot pink tank top and a short, and I mean short, mini skit. She quietly put her hand over my mouth as if to say, "Don't say anything." She opened the bedroom window and crawled out. Apparently, this was routine for her; I just happened to see it this time.

There is something to say about a mother's intuition; about five minutes later, my mom came into the room, went straight to the window, shut it, and locked it. She didn't say anything or look surprised to see the fake lump in my sister's bed made to represent a sleeping body. She just walked out of the room. Not only could I feel the disappointment, but I also saw it in her eyes.

There was another instance where sister number three [*the one with the Eddie Haskell Syndrome, consistently ingratiating herself to most adults and turning sinister around anyone else*] wanted to go to a wild party. I knew it was wild because all the kids at school were talking about it. By the way, Eddie Haskell was a character on an old black-and-white TV show called "Leave It to Beaver." Eddie was the friend of Beaver's old brother and was always getting into mischief.

I remember telling my sister, "Mom will never let you go to that party."

She replied, "Watch and learn, my sister, watch and learn." With her head held high and a slow, confident gait, she approached my mom. This angelic voice came from what I thought was my sister's mouth, but I didn't recognize it. She said, "Mom, this Friday, can I sleep over at Sharon's house?"

Sharon was her best friend and came from a structured home. My mom said, "If all your chores are done, I don't see why not."

When my sister returned to the room, she said, "See, I told you."

Thinking I had her, I responded, "You didn't ask to go to the party; you asked to go to a sleepover."

"Yee-UP," she replied, "but we will both be going to the party from there."

Puzzled, I pondered how they would pull it off. Later, I discovered it was the: tell each parent you are sleeping at a different friend's house, only to end up at the house of the friend whose parents didn't care what their kids did. The part I played was keeping my mouth shut if I was ever questioned. Oh, and my mom did find out when she received a phone call at about 12:30 a.m. from the police station to pick her little delinquent up. Pulling shenanigans like this, lying about everything, talking back, and fist-fighting at school and home were becoming the norm.

My sisters continued to push the envelope, with my mother constantly having her patience tried and tested. The frustration, sadness, and disappointment in her eyes were evident. With the drama from the divorce, dealing with her pain of being physically abused [sleeping with a knife under her pillow to protect herself if my dad came home drunk], working two jobs to provide enough to keep us out of a statistical low-income housing situation, and raising four girls without support, my mom had enough to worry about. At that moment, I was determined I would not be the cause of furthering her anguish. Whatever it took, I would be the "good kid" and protect my mother's heart.

Don't get it twisted; I was still human, flawed, and not the sinless saint of a child as it appeared. After witnessing three different ways [*from my siblings before me*] of doing things [*good, bad, and ugly*], I calculated and calibrated the precise way of getting away with the things that would, in an ordinary situation, receive punishment or bring pain to my mother. I'm not proud of this; it was just part of the plan to keep my mom's heart at peace. And it didn't stop there. I wanted her to be happy, and I felt that having some control in my life would give her peace to know that I wouldn't repeat mistakes and prevent me from being a statistic.

I would make decisions about my life, love, and situations based on what I thought would make my mom happy. I would seek her advice and approval for every significant move in my life. I remember fifth grade; that was the year students could join the band. You would meet with the band director, have lessons three times a week, and accompany the marching band during one of their performances. Once in seventh grade, you could officially march and perform with the band. The *"Pride of The Eastside"* is what they were often referred to. They were known for incorporating the most popular R&B or hip-hop songs with intricate routines in high-energy cultural showmanship and winning multiple concert awards. They were a well-respected, well-rounded organization, and I was super excited to have the chance to become a part of The Pride. Would I play the trumpet, flute, or saxophone, or explore other instrument possibilities? The choice was mine, or so I thought.

Running into the house and leaving the door wide open, I couldn't wait to tell my mom the great news. "Mom, Mom, Mom, I get to be in the band! I can pick any instrument -I think I want to play…"

My sentence was abruptly silenced. Mom, slightly startled, then decided for me to extinguish every ounce of excitement, remarked, "That's great; I think your cousin has an old clarinet you can use."

The pit of my stomach dropped. I would be that long, skinny girl hiding behind a long, skinny black horn. Rather than rock the boat, I accepted.

I was in a chemistry class -10th grade with Mr. Perkins, one of the quirkiest teachers one could imagine. If Albert Einstein were alive and 35, he would be his twin. Or, for the younger folks, he was oddly bizarre, like Bill Nye, the Science Guy. Science was my thing, like mixing math, biology, and chemistry concepts all in one. I read everything about chemistry and chemical properties I could find. It was the chemical reactions that sealed it for me. I wanted to research reactions from everything, from cleaning products to cosmetics, so I asked my mother to get me a junior chemistry set complete with a microscope, simple chemicals, glassware, and a crisp white lab coat and goggles.

Her response was, "Well, maybe for Christmas." I learned that phrase, and the phrase, "Well, wouldn't you rather wait until your birthday?" was what she would say to lessen the burden of saying 'no' because we couldn't afford it. Again, I chose to wait. When my birthday came and passed, I waited without discussion for Christmas - nothing. I dismissed the thought. She was probably right and should have made that decision for me earlier. I figured I needed to focus on another area besides science.

After my siblings moved out and started their adult lives, it was my time to apply for college. I chose to stay near home; I didn't want my mom to be sad or lonely. After all she had endured, I wanted to protect her heart.

I would intervene when others were rude or undependable or intercept phone calls or invitations from people who always wanted something other than friendship. I redirected the drama and neediness [even after they had moved out] that my siblings would inflict on my mom. If I handled the mess, it would save her the stress.

I *turned down out-of-state college acceptance and scholarships - the beginning of what* would soon be a conditioned response to avoid conflict, disappointment, and possible failure. I had already developed behavior reflexes, and the progression of my conformed compliance would begin to spill over into other areas of my life.

My mother also guided my choices as an adult, wife, and parent. I thought my compliance brought her joy, knowing I appreciated her words and understood all she tried to do as a single parent. I was pleased with my life yet also lost. How could I be lost if all my thoughts and decisions were met with approval? High approval at that, despite her failed marriage and life struggles. What I saw was a relentlessly strong, educated, and resilient woman. She made her way out of destruction and made a way for her girls.

In my continual interceding and compliance, I was uncomfortable making my decisions or challenging the status quo but had no problem when helping others. I was uncomfortable in the limelight, so I stayed in the background, mentoring, assisting, and supporting others at my job, at home, and with colleagues and friends.

Everyone would come to me with questions or problems, looking for a strategy or system to make things work. I became the "go-to person." I often heard, "If you want something done, take it to Kindred; she will make it happen." On any given day, I was drafting proposals, developing and organizing systems, and developing and presenting professional workshops—no recognition needed. I was more comfortable on the sidelines; High-recognition seats at the table were unavailable for people like me.

Once married, I took my mom's advice, "Do as the Lord says, honor your husband." I thought about why she would give me that advice. Was she talking about submission? Oh hell, nawh. If she did this, would that have prevented the abuse or divorce? To this day, I will never know. However, I interpreted that as acquiring *his* approval [respecting that I was married] for any decision I'd make.

Yeah, I know what you're thinking… mindless, controlling, subservient, well, not exactly, at least it didn't feel like it. I thought I was making everyone happy – and besides, he was happy, he loved me, he was a hard worker and an excellent provider. I was being harmonious; I was keeping the peace while sacrificing my own. We had two beautiful children – one girl and one boy – typical fairy tale life. Some would say our life together was Instagram-perfect. The reality is - you only post the good parts of life and leave out the everyday strife.

He would make final decisions about furniture, kitchen appliances, and décor, right down to the cookware. He chose the car I drove, and the job offer I should take. He weighed in on what type of clothes the kids wore, and he even attempted to buy me outfits he thought were "classy." Picture outfits designed for an old schoolteacher in the old western historical TV drama, *The Little House on Prairie*. When I asked for his opinion or included him in a decision, whether it be a new venture for me or changes in the house, it always ended in his favor. Why did I even ask? I was keeping the peace. I would respond, "It's okay; whatever you like is fine with me." Same response when making plans with friends, completing asks, or offering advice.

After years of this screeching broken record, "I'm fine, it's okay, no worries," I was at my limit. To my defense, I wasn't exactly a 'yes sir, yes ma'am' girl; more like I'd find positives in any situation. Instead of saying, "No, that is stupid," I would put an ingeniously positive spin on the idea, hoping they would see the light and not feel so dumb --I have a gift of problem-solving and systems. Instead of being a matter of fact, I was more concerned with how the person would feel if rejected. This behind-the-scenes go-to personality was getting old. I started to build up resentment, frustration, and loss of respect toward those who developed an overfamiliarity. Pleasing my mom, conforming to societal norms, and conceding to my spouse, I wanted to scream, f*** it all!

The frustration and stress began to show. In a resented agreement, my stomach would be tight and queasy, and I'd give the reaction of silence. I reacted reversely to stress; most people eat, but I could not. After going from a size 10/12 to a size 6, I knew something had to change. I was tired of being invisible and having my feelings ignored, but I did not know where or how to start. I spent the next three years consoling myself, thinking it was just my place in the world: put my big girl pants on, accept it, and keep it moving.

As time continued, more destruction of my mind, attitude, and actions surfaced. I became angry, depressed, and passive. This was compounded at home due to a lack of emotional support and the façade engrained in my spouse that 'everything was fine.' Did I create this? Did my mom induce this? My kids even noticed a change in my consensual ways that abruptly evolved into a 'don't make mom mad' attitude. I did all I could to suppress this; I didn't want my family disrupted. My daughter was about to graduate high school, and my son was entering ninth grade. I needed to pull it together, I repeated, as if an affirmation, "You're fine, life is good, you're good." I suppressed my feeling and kept it moving until…

It was the Christmas season; in two days, the kids would be out of school, my mom would share her recipes and yuletide for our annual Christmas Eve sleepover, and the festivities would begin. Christmas was always a happy time for me; I could decorate [my decisions/decor] and fill the house with all the trinkets and trimming everyone loved. My mom was always right there with me and traditionally had a gift exchange game where she read a Christmas story. But in the blink of an eye, the festivities were abruptly stifled.

And this is where I ended up in the fetal position, sobbing on the closet floor. It was December 24th after the funeral services for my mother [Christmas break would never be the same again.] Once I made it home, I was emotionally exhausted, overwhelmed, and depressed. I could not serve in my consistent capacity of making sure everyone else was okay. I retreated to my bedroom, escaping the constant flow of people and condolences. You see, it wasn't until my mom passed away that I realized I didn't know who I *really* was. God gives us a purpose and assignments. She was both. In fact, I loved protecting her emotionally and physically if needed. She gave me the emotional support and listening ear that I needed.

Suppressing the feelings of being invisible, not good enough, or the "yes, sir, ma'am," she made me feel seen and strong. However, years of doing what I thought made others happy or kept the peace only made me lose sight of who I was, what I liked, or what I wanted in life. I was lost. Without her, I felt like my purpose was gone. No one showed love and appreciation to me the way my mom did. After months of depression, counseling, and Xanax, I had to make a change. Now, it was clear, "Tomorrow may be too late."

She always said, "You are so talented. The world needs you." I realize I have talents and a creative spirit, but what would I do with them? I knew I had to find my passion and explore the things that would bring me joy. I needed a purpose. ***But what was I passionate about?*** I usually just helped others with their passions or projects; besides, it was safer in the background. I thought, ***how could I possibly move from putting others' happiness before my own? Is this selfish of me?*** *I was not only sad about losing my mom but also depressed because I had lost myself.*

It was time to awaken my inner being. I had to take action. Sitting quietly and allowing others to continue the same relationship with me had to end. I refer to James 2:26 (NIV), "Faith without works is dead." I needed to unveil who I was, and that would require action on my part. I had to take the advice, counseling, and mentoring I had done for others and use it for myself. I could no longer stay muted in the background. It was a slow process, one day at a time; I chipped away at the old me and began [in my mind and little responses and actions] preparing others around me for the new me coming. I would speak my mind and give the unbridled truths in conversations about situations that typically ended with me cowing down or saying yes when I meant no.

It was about six years after my mom passed before I could pick up my life and implement to the fullest the actions of my quest to find me. I started a daily routine of Bible time with meditation and devotion; from there, I read motivational books and studied mindfulness research and the psychology of the brain. My routine was good, but I needed more; the following year, I sought life coaching sessions. During the sessions, I felt heard and 'seen.' I began to explore my creativity with custom-crafted t-shirts and novelty items.

I needed mental distraction and a dose of confidence, so I enrolled at Northcentral University and sought a doctorate in Education Leadership. I hoped this would give me the courage to come off the sidelines, stand in front, and take the lead. I was determined to complete this degree and did so in three years. I knew my mom would have been proud. I could hear her say, "You are smart, beautiful, and can do anything you put your mind to." With that thought, I started daily affirmations and get-life-done lists (*aka* bucket lists in motion). I created a vision board and put everything I wanted to see, do, go, and achieve before me. Nothing was off limits. This was my board, and I did not need approval, nor was it up for discussion. I must say, I had bouts of anxiety when gluing down things like a 7-figure income, girls' trips out of the country, and becoming a best-seller published author, to name a few. The anxiety surfaced because I feared being judged or having my dreams devalued. I used gym time to relieve stress and anxiety, meditate, and take some me-time.

I began to embrace the things that resonated and put a smile in my heart, not just on my face. I have since redirected my life to Christ, earned a doctorate, and mapped out my retirement, or what I call my encore career. Problem-solving, listening, being innovative, and managing multiple situations and personalities is a gift that, once redirected, empowered me.

"You can't connect the dots looking forward; you can only connect them looking backwards."- Steve Jobs, former CEO of Apple. Meaning you must trust that the dots will somehow connect in your future. Trusting that my disconcerting childhood, submissive past, and the loss of my mom are what empowered and propelled me into my future self.

As I began to put change and action steps into play, it wasn't readily accepted by some. The patterns and routines that I had before were, in the eyes of others, changed abruptly. I would hear things like, *"Oooh, you're acting different,"* *"Why are you doing that?"* or *"What's wrong with you? Are you mad?"* and even the infamous Black woman epitome, *"Why so aggressive?"*

I was far from mad; I was confident, passionate, and straight-forward about what I was speaking or doing, not yielding an excuse or explanation for my decisions or statements. This wasn't easy; my anxiety surfaced during my first "no" conversation. I WAS a bit aggressive in reiterating my stance. My voice got loud, I rattled my point without breathing and snapped if I was questioned. I have since redirected that energy and realized I don't have to feel guilty about what I need, nor help anyone understand it. My "yes" meant yes, and my "no" meant no. No excuse, no justification, just the decision.

When others would speak about their life [listening is one of my best qualities] this time around, I would simply listen and acknowledge their struggle. The old me would have given up my time to assist or taken control completely.

As I reflect on my motives and movement, I had to change my behavior to change the behavior of others, showing them how to respect and treat me. How could I do this so assuredly? Think about it; it's like housebreaking a puppy; instead of sleeping in, I have to get up, get moving, and take the puppy outside to do his business. If I choose to remain in bed or sleep, the puppy will continue his natural behavior of relieving himself regardless. So, you see, changing your behavior to get the expected results. The philosophy I live by [for now] is reciprocity. As a woman, wife, colleague, or friend, I show up, respond, treat you how I want to be treated, and then wait and observe. Lack of reciprocity places our friendship in a different category of acquaintances, significance, or an as-needed basis. Sometimes, you must eliminate the excess baggage to progress or move with ease. God said to love everyone, and I do. In 1 Thessalonians 2:4 (NLT), he also said that we are to work for others as servants of God, not as people-pleasers.

My journey is far from over, but I have finally begun to understand and embrace my authentic self. Now, I make decisions based on what brings me joy and do things for others because I want to, not because it's what they would expect or because I'm trying to make them happy or seek validation and approval. I move with peace and confidence.

I reflect on the words of Cheryl Polote-Williamson, a dear friend and motivational speaker who would say, *"Validation is for parking, not for people; God validated you when you were born."* I can now recognize and accept my internal experiences, thoughts, and feelings. Thus, a stronger self-identity, questionless decision-making, and actions with confidence. As I continue to find myself and grow, I've realized that the only person I need to ensure happiness is me, and the only approval I need is from God. To hear Him say, as stated in Romans 12:2 (NIV), *"Do not conform to the pattern of the world but be transformed by the renewing of your mind. Then you will be able to recognize and identify what God's will is - his good, pleasing, and perfect will."*

Reflection

Looking back at your childhood, what is the most significant occurrence you will always remember? *(positive or negative)*

How important are you to yourself?

What impact have you made in your life or in the lives of others? *(positive or negative)*

An Affirmative Prayer

With faith as my guide, I honor God's will and plan for my life. I am at peace with the things that I cannot control. I welcome His abundant blessings and know that I am worthy of love and acceptance just as I am. My thoughts create my reality – I am careful with my words or thoughts about myself.

I embrace my unique qualities and let go of comparisons. I release self-doubt and believe in my limitless potential. Through the love of Christ, I deserve happiness and fulfillment in every aspect of my life!

"The Lord is near to the brokenhearted and saves the crushed in spirit." Psalm 34:18 (KJV)

"My flesh and my heart faileth: but God is the strength of my heart, and my portion forever." Psalm 73:26 (KJV)

"Blessed are they that mourn: for they shall be comforted." Matthew 5:4 (KJV)

Just Write

Bibliography

Oglesby-Henry, Rosemary. (2022) *The Rose Who Blossomed Through the Concrete Consequence vs Choice.* Santa Ana, CA: Trilogy Christian Publishing.